Praise for *Animals, Disability, and the End of Capitalism*

"This book adds to the growing literature on eco-ability, adding a number of new voices to the conversation. Drawing on diverse theoretical perspectives and firsthand experience, the authors in this collection make clear the connections between ableism and speciesism."

Constance Russell, professor at Lakehead University

"This important contribution to political resistance in the era of Trump calls for nothing short of total liberation. As the Earth shrieks in its descent into oblivion, and the vast majority of its inhabitants prepare themselves for the slaughter bench of history, the activists in this volume chart a different course, one that needs our attention now, more than at any previous time.... It's a book that demands to be read."

Peter McLaren, author of *Pedagogy of Insurrection*

"*Animals, Disability, and the End of Capitalism* is a key book to move the earth and animal liberation movements to be more inclusive and complex with their goals and analysis. This rich read offers any social justice activist a holistic understanding of intersectionality."

Carolyn Drew, Institute for Critical Animal Studies

"Having spent many years campaigning with my wife, Louise, who is a wheelchair user, for both animal liberation and the rights of people with disabilities, I am delighted to see this book."

Ronnie Lee, founder of the Animal Liberation Front

"Highly original in both content and ambition, *Animals, Disability, and the End of Capitalism* makes a tremendously powerful and timely contribution to the literature. Accessible and inspiring, this book deserves to be read—and re-read—widely. It should certainly be embraced by critical scholars and activists alike, but, in the final analysis, this is a book that speaks to everyone who desires a better world, based on freedom and justice for each and all.

Richard J. White, Reader in Human Geography, Sheffield Hallam University, UK

"The eco-ability movement and this book in particular give both practical (and theoretical) insight in that total liberation is much more than mere intersectionality: Ableism (towards humans) and speciesism don't intersect at all, but still the exchange between both perspectives, the learning from each other and the co-operation and combination of both struggles and strugglers make a lot of sense and are highly beneficial, if not an absolute necessity to true liberatory success of any of these struggles."

Jörg Hartmann, Regional Representative, Institute for Critical Animal Studies, Europe

Animals, Disability, and the End of Capitalism

RADICAL ANIMAL STUDIES AND TOTAL LIBERATION

Anthony J. Nocella II
Series Editor

Vol. 1

The Radical Animal Studies and Total Liberation series
is part of the Peter Lang Education list.
Every volume is peer reviewed and meets
the highest quality standards for content and production.

PETER LANG
New York • Bern • Berlin
Brussels • Vienna • Oxford • Warsaw

Animals, Disability, and the End of Capitalism

Voices from the Eco-ability Movement

Edited by Anthony J. Nocella II,
Amber E. George, and John Lupinacci

PETER LANG
New York • Bern • Berlin
Brussels • Vienna • Oxford • Warsaw

Library of Congress Cataloging-in-Publication Data

Names: Nocella, Anthony J., editor.
George, Amber E., editor. | Lupinacci, John, editor.
Title: Animals, disability, and the end of capitalism: voices from the
eco-ability movement / edited by Anthony J. Nocella II,
Amber E. George, and John Lupinacci.
Description: New York: Peter Lang, 2019.
Series: Radical animal studies and total liberation; vol. 1
ISSN 2469-3065 (print) | ISSN 2469-3081 (online)
Includes bibliographical references and index.
Identifiers: LCCN 2018017572 | ISBN 978-1-4331-3516-3 (hardback: alk. paper)
ISBN 978-1-4331-3515-6 (paperback: alk. paper)
ISBN 978-1-4331-5741-7 (ebook pdf) | ISBN 978-1-4331-5742-4 (epub)
ISBN 978-1-4331-5743-1 (mobi)
Subjects: LCSH: Disability studies. | Animal welfare.
Social justice. | Human ecology.
Classification: LCC HV1568.2.A55 2018 | DDC 362.4—dc23
LC record available at https://lccn.loc.gov/2018017572
DOI 10.3726/b14134

Bibliographic information published by **Die Deutsche Nationalbibliothek**.
Die Deutsche Nationalbibliothek lists this publication in the "Deutsche
Nationalbibliografie"; detailed bibliographic data are available
on the Internet at http://dnb.d-nb.de/.

© 2019 Peter Lang Publishing, Inc., New York
29 Broadway, 18th floor, New York, NY 10006
www.peterlang.com

All rights reserved.
Reprint or reproduction, even partially, in all forms such as microfilm,
xerography, microfiche, microcard, and offset strictly prohibited.

This book is dedicated to all those that are incarcerated, imprisoned, caged, chained, restrained, medicated, tortured, and murdered because they are different and have disabilities.

Table of Contents

Acknowledgments	ix
Foreword JUDY K.C. BENTLEY	xi
Introduction: Defending and Sharing Space and Place for Eco-ability Voices for Total Liberation ANTHONY J. NOCELLA II, AMBER E. GEORGE, AND JOHN LUPINACCI	1
1. *Critical Animal Studies and the Importance of Anti-Racist and Anti-Ableist Politics* ANTHONY J. NOCELLA II, AMBER E. GEORGE, JOHN LUPINACCI, AND MENEKA REPKA	9
2. *The Interdependency of Humans and Nature: A Plea for Ecopedagogy and Eco-ability Activism* SARAH R. ADAMS	25
3. *From Collective Autism to Autistic Wildness* DANIEL SALOMON	39
4. *I Fled to the Wilderness and Was Surprised by Enlightenment* DANIEL SALOMON	51
5. *Post-Structural Analyses of Conformity and Oppression: A Discussion of Critical Animal Studies and Neurodiversity* HANNAH MONROE	59
6. *Giving a Face to the Nameless Numbers* MARY FANTASKE	71

7. *Reframing Companion Animal Disability Using the Social Model:*
   Removing Barriers and Facilitating Care   81
   NICOLE R. PALLOTTA

8. *Seeding Ableism*   103
   AVA HABERKORNHALM

9. *Dealing with Trauma Holistically: Introducing Eco-ability*
   Liberatory Therapy   111
   MARISSA ANDERSON

Contributors   121

Index   125

Acknowledgments

John, Amber, and Anthony would like to thank all the contributors of this book, as well as Carmen Dell'Aversano, Jovian Parry, Rasmus Rahbek Simonsen, Daniel Salomon, Zach Richter, Sunaura Taylor, Amy J. Fitzgerald, Lauren Corman, Matthew Ross Calarco, Maneesha Dechha, Amie Breeze Harper, Erika Cudworth, Kathryn Asher, Elizabeth Cherry, Carmen Cusack, Claudia Serrato, Adam J. Fix, and A. O. Owoseni. We would like to thank everyone with the amazing and outstanding Peter Lang Publishing, especially Sarah, Tim, Chris, and Sophie. We would also like to thank Judy K.C. Bentley for her Foreword and dedication to helping develop the field of eco-ability and critical animal studies. Without her support and involvement in the Institute for Critical Animal Studies (ICAS), it would not be where it is today. We would also like to thank the ICAS and everyone with and supportive of ICAS—Lara Drew, Carolyn Drew, Sean Parson, Ian Purdy, Carol Mendoza, Mari Anderson, Richard White, Erik Juergensmeyer, Judy K. C. Bentley, Janet Duncan, Mecke Nagel, Peter McLaren, Richard Kahn, Sinem Ketenci, JL Schatz, Scott Hurley, Helena Pedersen, Vasile Stănescu, Stephanie Eccles, Kaden Maguire, Mara Pfeffer, Jess Ison, Les Mitchell, Aragorn Eloff, John Sorenson, John Alessio, Julie Andrzejewski, Sarah Smith, Colleen Mollentze, Luis Cordeiro-Rodrigues, Andrea Marais-Potgieter, Jörg Hartmann, Carlos García, Daniela Romero Waldorn, Alexandra Navarro, María Marta Andreatta, Gabriela Anahí González, Cassiana Lopes Stephan, Eduardo Rincón Higuer, Iván Darío Ávila Gaitán, Fernando Bottom, Colin Salter, Samuel León Martínez, Ariadna Beiroz, Andrea Padilla Villarraga, Carlos Andrés Moreno Urán, Bogna Konior, Sara Tsui, rocky Schwartz, Daniel Frank, and Terry Hurtado. We would also like to thank Save the Kids, Poetry Behind the Walls, Wisdom Behind the Walls, Institute for Hip Hop Activism, Outdoor Empowerment, *Peace Studies Journal, Transformative Justice Journal, Green*

Theory and Praxis Journal, Total Liberation Working Group at Northern Arizona University, Department of Sociology at Fort Lewis College, Eco-ability Collective, Durango Peace and Justice, Durango Hip Hop, National Week of Action Against Incarcerating Youth, Arissa Media Group, POPS Movement, FLC Black Student Union, FLC Sociology Club, FLC Criminology Club, Durango ADAPT, Durango Animal Liberation, Durango Veg Fest, Chris Mendoza, Kim Socha, David Gabbard, Becky Clausen, Keri Brandt, Mark Seis, Janine Fitzgerald, Kate Smith, Carey Vicenti, FLC Environmental Studies, FLC Education Program, FLC Peace and Conflict Studies, FLC Gender and Women's Studies, Carolina Alonso, Kathy Fine, Emily Houghton, Michael Martin, Janneli Miller, Cory Pillen, Sarah Roberts-Cady, Amy Sellin, Natasha Tidwell, Laurel Baldwin, Dawn Widen, and Michael Fry. We would also like to thank most importantly our families. John would like to acknowledge the human and nonhuman members of his family, the students and faculty in the Cultural Studies and Social Thought program at Washington State University, the radical activists sacrificing life and freedom for liberation, and all of the radical activist-educators fighting in classrooms and communities to abolishing normalcy. Amber would like to thank her friends, family her husband Jacob Gindi, children Aviva, Ezra, and Isabelle, and cats Abby and Simi and everyone in ICAS.

Foreword

JUDY K.C. BENTLEY

The academic discipline of disability studies in education began with a critical analysis of traditional "special" education, fueled by emotional confrontation and courageous scrutiny of so-called "inclusive" practices in our public schools. After a decade of exposing and actively contesting the re-segregation of students with disabilities by labeling, low expectations, and "special" segregated classes, disability studies scholar-activists have established a liberatory movement that is changing the way we teach and learn. While we need further exploration of the likely influence of disability studies on changes in attitude, understanding and quest for true belonging of students with other discriminated differences in our education system—and while their belonging is currently challenged even more in the current push for school "choice"—the movement and its goals are strong and effective.

The Eco-ability movement began with a conversation I had with Anthony Nocella about disability studies in education, and how its context had sometimes been misinterpreted to re-segregate and re-oppress the individuals it was meant to empower. Various academic departments and professional conferences seemed at that time to "specialize" in disability, and attempt to "own" it, so that it was deemed inappropriate for other departments to study and share knowledge about disability as a lived experience. Disability studies faculty were often called on merely to supply the "disability angle" (too often misconstrued as a deficit-based medical model) in a conversation, presentation, or manuscript. With a desire to communicate the real mission and vision of disability studies in education, we agreed that the word "ability" was more descriptive of the (dis)ability studies movement, free from the existential and semantic "dis" that held it down.

Deficit labeling, low expectations, segregation, and the damage they can do are not unique to disability. The same misguided and oppressive constructs affect all human and nonhuman animals, and the environment as well. This perspective led us to apply the concept of "intersectionality," (Crenshaw, 1991), the idea that oppressive paradigms (personal and environmental racism, ableism, sexism, speciesism) are interrelated, and must not be analyzed apart from one another.

With the publication of *Earth, Animal and Disability Liberation: The Rise of the Eco-Ability Movement* (2012), Eco-ability became a movement and a nascent field of academic study. New voices and new disciplines were invited to collaborate in an intersectional exchange of information and experience and a call for social justice. Eco-ability promotes a social justice theory and movement that deconstructs "normalcy," troubles hierarchies of "worth," and fosters mutual interdependence, collaboration, and respect for difference, in a fully inclusive world.

Quite soon, scholar-activists Colin Salter, Amber George, and J. L. Schatz joined us to produce subsequent volumes: *Animals and War: Confronting the Military-Industrial-Animal Complex* (2014), *Screening the Nonhuman: Representations of Animal Others in the Media* (2016), and *The Intersectionality of Critical Animal, Disability, and Environmental Studies: Toward Eco-ability, Justice and Liberation* (2017).

This book, *Animal, Disability, and Earth Liberation Activists for Total Liberation: Voices from the Eco-ability Movement* propels and exemplifies the core values of the Eco-ability movement, with a focus on activism. The editors—Anthony Nocella, Amber George and John Lupinacci—have assembled a community of bright and committed new scholars, with fresh ideas and an unwavering commitment to advocacy for change. *Animal, Disability, and Earth Liberation Activists for Total Liberation: Voices from the Eco-ability Movement* is their first published work. They are nearly all vegans; and they bring lived experience with social injustice and (dis)ability to their remarkable and deeply personal stories.

Through their leadership in the field of Eco-ability, the editors continue to mentor and support new generations of the movement. Anthony is an intersectional, collaborative social justice scholar, educator, and activist with an international reputation. Amber teaches social philosophy, and serves as an ally, counselor, and community educator in social justice administration. John teaches and advocates for the development of scholar-activist educators.

Animal, Disability, and Earth Liberation Activists for Total Liberation: Voices from the Eco-ability Movement invites the discerning reader to meet the same challenges required of the authors—to name and look beyond one's own privilege, to recognize and explore indignity, injustice, and subjugation, and to work toward transformative justice. Know that you will find here a book by scholar-activists whose words will leave you hopeful, stronger, and better prepared to make a difference.

References

Crenshaw, K. (1991, July). Mapping the margins: Intersectionality, identity politics, and violence against women of color. *Stanford Law Review*, *43*(6), 1241–1299. doi:10.2307/1229039

George, A., & Schatz, J. L. (Eds.). (2016). *Screening the Nonhuman: Representations of animal others in the media*. Lanham, MD: Lexington.

Nocella, A., Bentley, J. K. C., & Duncan, J. (Eds.). (2012). *Earth, animal and disability liberation: The rise of the eco-ability movement*. New York, NY: Peter Lang Publishing.

Nocella, A., George, A., & Schatz, J. L. (Eds.). (2017). *The intersectionality of critical animal, disability, and environmental studies: Toward eco-ability, justice and liberation*. Lanham, MD: Lexington.

Nocella, A., Salter, C., & Bentley, J. K. C. (Eds.). (2014). *Animals and war: Confronting the military-industrial-animal complex*. Lanham, MD: Lexington.

Introduction: Defending and Sharing Space and Place for Eco-ability Voices for Total Liberation

Anthony J. Nocella II, Amber E. George, and John Lupinacci

As part of the recent growth in diverse scholar-activism, eco-ability addresses the importance of recognizing disability as having differing abilities and theories of ability that contribute to a more holistic and inclusive understanding of diversity. Furthermore, eco-ability scholarship emerging with, and from, critical animal studies (CAS) works from an anti-speciesist definition of diversity that suggests value in the many ways we all exist and contribute as interrelated and interdependent beings. Far too often, social justice work is not only human centered at the expense of nonhumans but is also policed by assumptions that stem from a problematic baseline of human-being as being one particular thing—a consuming, white, heterosexual, cis gendered, male, presenting with no disabilities or anything that may differentiate an individual from a universalizing image and identity. Referring to this as normalcy, critical scholars have exposed the social dangers of such a way of existing as being in any way normal.

Challenging labels and categories of who can speak truth to experience, eco-ability scholarship seeks to include all voices, especially the voices of those for whom voice isn't simply limited to words or standard conventions of academic writing. Resisting the disciplining of normalcy, eco-ability is defined by Nocella (2012) the "theory that nature, nonhuman animals, and people with disabilities promote collaboration, not competition; interdependency, not independence; and respect for difference and diversity, not sameness and normalcy" (p. 9). Sarat Collings (2012) challenges the borders of normalcy and nation, emphasizing the potential in the anarchist concept of mutual aid, explains that "eco-ability is based on Nature's teaching of diversity" (p. 92) and challenges the monoculturalizing of diversity endemic of systems of global capitalism. Collings (2012) notes that while disability scholars suggest that considering the ethics of the body ought to start with the unstable category of *disability* it is also important to include the category of animal, or Nature. Eco-ability scholarship recognizes that the degradation of marginalized people, especially persons with any of a multitude of possible disabilities, is deeply connected to the accepted domination and subjugation of nonhuman. To this extent, eco-ability work seeks to bring together diverse scholars sharing how they experience disability and resist the policing exclusionary violence of normalcy.

This book is the third book that discusses the eco-ability movement using diverse essays to further examine the complexity of normalcy, diversity, and anthropocentrism. Furthermore, this book provides space and place for diverse eco-ability activist perspectives often excluded from academic publications. Many of the authors in this book not only have disabilities, but also have not been published before despite their many years of experience recognizing and resisting ableism and other forms of exclusionary violence. These voices are the primary sources for research and offer insight that expose problematic assumptions often made by even the most critical of social justice activists and scholars. Most of the time in scholarly and academic texts, we learn from detached scholars that are not affected directly by systemic forms of oppression and this is especially the case with scholarship confronting ableism. The authors in this book tell their stories, share perceptions, and impart thoughts in relation to their unique life stories, all of which draws from practices of autoethnography and feminist standpoint theory.

Autoethnography in Eco-ability

Many writings by bell hooks are located in her socio-economic political identity and personal experiences, a method known as autoethnography. Other famous activist autoethnographies include, *The Story of My Life: The Restored Edition* (Keller, 2004), *Autobiography of Malcolm X* (X & Haley, 1965), *Gandhi An Autobiography: The Story of My Experiments with Truth* (Gandhi & Desai, 1993), *A Child Called "It": One Child's Courage to Survive* (Pelzer, 1995), and *Long Walk to Freedom: The Autobiography of Nelson Mandela* (Mandela, 2000). These are just a few of the many autoethnographies that interweave personal narrative with theory and action. Methodologists who promote autoethnography argue that research can be conducted successfully on a topic through first-person narratives that relate action with the ideas and self-reported motives of the individual.

Unfortunately, autoethnography is a methodology that has not been used a great deal in the social sciences when compared with other methodologies (Russell, 1999). While autoethnography provides rich data, it blurs the role of researcher and subject (Ferrell & Hamm, 1998), which is also a goal and purpose of activist methodology. Therefore, to take the researcher out of this project is to lose an important part of the story. We encouraged our contributing authors to use personal experiences because we believe it expands the scope of information available. Thus, this collection includes autobiographies, poems, personal story-telling, narratives, testimony, and other forms of communication that examine the experience of the researcher/author. We feel this type of scholarship is integral to being inclusive and disruptive to the status quo, particularly when it comes to disability perspectives. In the case of people with disabilities,

> ...narratives of illness have the power to transform both the author and the audience: They serve to both inform the public about illness phenomenon and clarify and affirm the experience for the person who experiences it. In the field of psychiatric research, consumer narratives are increasingly recognized as an invaluable resource for understanding the perspectives of people who have experienced mental illness firsthand or in their immediate families and for raising consciousness about appropriate forms of treatment. (Corrigan, 2006, p. 69)

Autoethnography differs from the recognition of personality in research (that is, the notion that the researcher's reflections, feelings, and biases influence the research process) because the researcher's personal experiences—as expressed in a variety of ways—serve as a key data set for analysis.

Feminist Standpoint Theory

Similar to autoethnography, feminist standpoint methodology, was developed by a number of feminists including Sandra Harding (1998), Donna Haraway (1991), and Nancy Hartsock (1997). Feminist standpoint methodology is a form of perspectival theory/methodology. Central to influencing feminist standpoint theory was Friedrich Nietzsche's ((1977; 2017) understanding of metaphysics in which he argued that there are no facts, only interpretations, and that all interpretations are shaped by one's perspectives and thus are laden with presuppositions and biases. Nietzsche argued the more perspectives one could draw from, the more one could better understand reality. Thus, to avoid the falsehoods and simplicities associated with mono-perspectival approaches, Nietzsche urged that one should employ a *variety* of perspectives and interpretations (Nietzsche, 1977; 2017). Two crucial points come out of Nietzsche's discussion that became crucial for feminist standpoint theory: first, the knowledge we have is always limited and partial; second, all knowledge is influenced by a number of factors, which include one's presuppositions, but also one's existential, social, and identity standpoint including factors such as one's class, racial, and gender position. For our purposes in this book, we'd also add many other social and species identities such as one's nonhuman and disability status. Furthermore, feminists recognized that Nietzsche was somewhat limited in his view as a male, so they expanded beyond his metaphysics to include distinctive female points of view. According to Sandra Harding, "for almost two decades feminists have engaged in a complex and charged conversation about objectivity" (cited in Alcoff and Potter p. 49). Ezzy writes, "Feminist standpoint epistemologies reject the modernist assumption that there is a single ideal knower and that he (it is typically a male) can know or describe one true and final correct representation or reality" (Ezzy, 2002, p. 20). Like feminists, the eco-ability authors included in this text contribute the perspectives of nonhumans, Nature, and people with disabilities in to this discussion. We recognize that knowledge is based on experience and socio-political values and therefore all our contributions to the field of eco-ability are shaped by our experiences and life lenses. Accordingly, "we must acknowledge that different researcher identities generate different insights and that a diversity of researcher identities thus opens avenues into a diversity of research settings and understanding" (Ferrell & Hamm, 1998, p. 256).

In this text, we challenge assumptions of the objectivist modernist theory and methodology that research can and should be neutral and detached, which is itself not a true or ahistorical claim but rather a social construction that should be deconstructed (DeVault, 1999; Evans, 1980; Ezzy, 2002). Thomas Kuhn was one ardent critic of objectivist modernist science and truth-seeking. In Kuhn's 1962 classic, *The Structure of Scientific Revolutions*, he rejected the entire model of scientific knowledge as an internal logic that steadily progresses along the path of "truth," to argue that knowledge is organized in a series of changing "paradigms" that are merely different from one another and do not "progress" toward Truth. Kuhn replaced an "internal" model of knowledge from an "external" approach that emphasized the social and historical influences on science. Kuhn's work helped to expose the fraud whereby scientists hide behind the "certainty" of "objective" practice with a set of rigid set beliefs, which by default structures a particular outcome, rather than one that is free and uninfluenced. Scientific theories and paradigms are directly and/or directly governed and influenced by the dominant religious, political, economic, cultural ideologies of a given society. Objectivity and the modernist mania for quantitative measurement, for instance, creates racist and ableist theories and approaches such as eugenics, IQ testing, and standardized tests. Along with feminists, critical theorists, critical race theorists, postcolonialists, postmodernists, anarchists, Marxists, disability theorists, and queer theorists, the eco-ability authors in this text are contributing to expanding Kuhn's ideas and challenging the core dogmas of Western theory and modernist epistemology.

Further, quite unlike the isolated, detached, and political knower of modern epistemology, feminist standpoint methodology is based on shared experiences and concerns about oppressed and repression communities and group (Ezzy, 2002). Like feminist standpoint methodology, eco-ability also examines history written "from below." Taking their cue from Marxist and populist theories that focus on the struggles of peasants, serfs, and urban working classes, our authors recover the voices of various marginalized groups silenced by conventional history as well as the reductionist class struggle narrative of Marxist theory. Harding writes,

> standpoint theorists themselves all explicitly argue that marginal lives that are not their own provide better grounds for certain kind of knowledge. Thus the claim by women that women's lives provide a better starting point for thoughts about gender systems is not the same as the claim that their own lives are the best such starting points. (Alcoff & Potter, 1993, p. 58)

This text emerges from a call from oppressed and marginalized communities demanding resistance against modernist, speciesist, anthropocentric, Eurocentric, racist, sexist, and capitalist, socially constructed notions of "objectivity." Like critical pedagogy, eco-ability is a *praxis*; it rejects the modernist ideals of knowledge as objective, nonpartisan, nonbiased, and detached because it has a strong commitment to understanding the oppressed and working for liberation of all, human and nonhuman alike. We seek to not only to understand the conditions of oppressed groups and peoples, but also to be immersed in their struggles. We also demand that the products of our work, such as the writing of this book, be practical. As a result, this methodology goes to the root of the problem and examines the macro socio-political problem of domination and oppression, developed by social construction of "privilege." At the same time, however, this approach demands that researchers understand their privilege and how they oppress; it forces the individual to take ownership of their actions and perspectives, which potentially oppress others in some ways, despite their intentions to develop a liberatory politics and praxis.

Outline of the Book

In chapter one, "Critical Animal Studies and the Importance of Anti-Racist and Anti-Ableist Politics," Anthony J. Nocella II, Amber E. George, John Lupinacci, and Meneka Repka give an overview of the close relationship between the personal and political dimensions and tensions of working together in an activist network focused on addressing and better understanding the relationship between species, racism, and ableism. Sharing a glimpse into the work they are doing as part of belonging to the Institute for Critical Animal Studies (ICAS), Nocella et al. propose the idea that there may be a need for a radical animal studies—a critical extension of CAS that works at the intersections of race, ability, and speciesism toward an Anti-Racist and Anti-Ableist politics.

Sarah Adams in chapter two, "The Interdependency of Humans and Nature: A Plea for Ecopedagogy and Eco-ability Activism," explores the concept of ecotherapy and ecopedgogy as a way of reciprocal healing of the self and the Earth. Adams recounts the lessons she learned about the importance of eco-pedagogy in conjunction with eco-ability while protesting the construction of the Dakota Access pipeline at the Standing Rock Reservation in North Dakota.

In chapter three "From Collective Autism to Autistic Wildness" and chapter four "I Fled to the Wilderness and Was Surprised by Enlightenment," writing in his preferred voice, Daniel Solomon shares the connection between deep ecology, ecofeminism, and Rachel Carson's Silent Spring as he visits that place where Carson wrote that seminal book. Solomon explores the conflict between the neurodiversity and deep ecology movements to determine how to best resolve the conflict through interest-based conflict resolution.

In chapter five "Post-Structural Analyses of Conformity and Oppression: A Discussion of Critical Animal Studies and Neurodiversity," Hannah Monroe explores the discursive construction of normative behavior and non-conformity. Monroe discuss theories about normativity from a post-structural perspective, this chapter focuses on critical disability theory and describes the discursive processes of medicalization focusing on neurodiversity and autism.

Mary Fantaske in chapter six, "Giving a Face to the Nameless Numbers" examines the systematic ways "ability diverse humyns" are oppressed via ableism and speciesism. Highlight similarities between ableism and speciesism, Fantaske, noting the number of similarities, makes a strong argument for the joint combatting of ableism and speciesism through an ecofeminist "ethics of care" and "bearing witness."

In chapter seven, "Reframing Companion Animal Disability Using the Social Model: Removing Barriers and Facilitating Care," Nicole R. Pallotta explores the issues surrounding providing care for companion animals with disabilities. She discusses various improvements that could be made in human society to remove systemic barriers that impede animals with disabilities from receiving quality assistance. Pallotta uses her personal experience caring for a disabled canine family member to examine broader social issues that impact accessibilty and care.

In chapter eight, "Seeding Ableism," Ava HaberkornHalm provides a critical overview of inclusive gardens and argues that even with many activist's effort to adhere to an ADA framework community gardens are far from inclusive. Touching on important intersections between access to healthy food and ones right to being part of the production, preparation, and consumption of food, HaberkornHalm, invites gardeners and activists to commit to inclusive community gardens and shares suggestions for doing so.

In chapter nine, Marissa Anderson's essay, "Dealing with Trauma Holistically: Introducing Eco-ability Liberatory Therapy" explores how an eco-ability focused treatment plan can help liberate people with disabilities while at the same time fostering a respect for Nature. Using various aspects of her intersectional identity as a feminist with disabilities, a vegan, an anarchist, a Hip Hop activist, and a defender of the earth and all its inhabitants, she discusses how liberation for and by the environment is a key component to her life.

Operating with a far broader concept of knowledge than allowed by positivist science or philosophy, eco-ability fosters and supports narratives and story-telling (Alcoff, 2003; Church, 1995; James, 2005; Mugo, 1991). Like bell hooks (1989), our text strives to discover personal stories as well as to consciously and deliberately promote liberation (Ferrell & Hamm, 1998). Eco-ability is based on shared experiences and concerns about oppressed and repression communities and group and promotes a diversity of voices.

References

Alcoff, L. M. (2003). *Singing in the fire: Stories of women in philosophy*. New York, NY: Rowman and Littlefield.
Alcoff, L. M., & Potter, E. (1993). *Feminist epistemologies*. New York, NY: Routledge.
Church, K. (1995). *Forbidden narratives: Critical autobiography as social science*. New York, NY: Routledge.
Collings, S. (2012). Transnational feminism and eco-ability: Transgressing the borders of normalcy and nation. In A. J. Nocella, J. K. C. Bentley, & J. M. Duncan (Eds.), *Earth,*

animal, and disability liberation: the rise of the eco-ability movement (pp. 91–107). New York, NY: Peter Lang Publishing.

Corrigan, P. W. (2006). *On the stigma of mental illness: Practical strategies for research and social change.* Washington, DC: American Psychological Association.

Ezzy, D. (2002). *Qualitative analysis.* New York, NY: Routledge.

Ferrell, J., & Hamm, M. S. (1998). *Ethnography at the edge: Crime, deviance, and field research.* Boston, MA: Northeastern University Press.

Gandhi, M. K., & Desai, M. (1993). *Gandhi an autobiography: The story of my experiments.* New York, NY: Dover Publications Inc.

Haraway, D. (1991). A cyborg manifesto: Science, technology, and socialist-feminism in the late twentieth century. In S. Stryker & S. Whittle (Eds.), *The transgender studies reader.* New York, NY: Routledge

Harding, S. (1998). *Is science multicultural? Postcolonialism, feminism, and epistemologies.* Bloomington, IN: Indiana University Press.

Hartsock, N. C. M. (1997). *The feminist standpoint revisited & other essays.* Boulder, CO: Westview Press.

hooks, b. (1989). *Talking back: Thinking feminist thinking black.* Boston, MA: South End Press.

James, J. (2005). *The new abolitionists: (Neo) slave narratives and contemporary prison writings.* Albany, NY: SUNY Press.

Keller, H. (2004). *The story of my life: The restored edition.* Hollywood, FL: Simon & Brown.

Kuhn, T. (1962). *The structure of scientific revolution.* Chicago, IL: Chicago University Press.

Mandela, N. (2000). *Long walk to freedom: The autobiography of Nelson Mandela.* Chicago, IL: Steck-Vaughn.

Mugo, M. M. G. (1991). *African orature and human rights.* Institute of Southern African Studies National University of Lesotho.

Nietzsche, F. (1977). *The portable Nietzsche* (W. Kaufmann, Trans.). New York, NY: Viking Press.

Nietzsche, F. (2017). *The will to power.* London: Penguin.

Pelzer, D. J. (1995). *A child called "It": One child's courage to survive.* Deerfield, FL: HCI.

Russell, C. (1999). *Experiential ethnography.* Durham, NC: Duke University Press.

X, M., & Haley, A. (1965). *Autobiography of Malcolm X.* New York, NY: Grove Press.

1. Critical Animal Studies and the Importance of Anti-Racist and Anti-Ableist Politics

Anthony J. Nocella II, Amber E. George, John Lupinacci, and Meneka Repka

Locating Ourselves

As scholar-activists committed to Critical Animal Studies (CAS), we are working collaboratively on diverse fronts to radically transform the dominant systems that undermine social justice and sustainability. In keeping with feminist standpoint theory, we would like to introduce ourselves as we refer to individual experiences and wish to provide context for our perspectives. Anthony, a professor with a doctorate from the U.S., identifies as a white, able-bodied man, with disabilities and queer. An active participant and founder of the Institute for Critical Studies, he is also a coordinator with Save the Kids—a national U.S. fully-volunteer grass-roots group with over eleven chapters that work to end police brutality. He is also involved with Black Lives Matter, ending the incarceration of youth, prison abolition, the school-to-prison pipeline, and Hip Hop activism through sit-ins, die-ins, rallies, workshops, teach-ins, community circles, protests and highway and street takeovers. Johnny, a professor with a doctorate in education, identifies as a scholar-activist educator working at the intersections of social and ecological justice while recognizing his privileges as a white male heterosexual relatively able-bodied human working to interrupt the social reproduction of oppression and suffering in schools. Amber, a professor and administrator with a doctorate in philosophy is a white, heterosexual woman, with disability, and an English-speaking U.S. citizen who conducts workshops, dialogues, conference presentations, and protests for non/human and human liberation. Meneka, with a doctorate in education, is a college instructor, high school teacher, and activist and identifies as a Brown, Canadian, cisgender, heterosexual woman who, like Johnny, is working to challenge and resist the implicit and explicit inequities that are present in educational spaces. In this chapter, we share our perspectives on the importance of anti-ableist and anti-racist politics in partnership and solidarity with CAS.

What Is Critical Animal Studies?

The best place to find the most detailed history of CAS is in the introduction of *Defining Critical Animals: An Intersectional Social Justice Approach for Liberation* (Nocella II, Sorenson, Socha, & Matsuoka, 2014). According to the Institute for Critical Animal Studies (ICAS), which aided in co-founding the field, CAS is:

> rooted in animal liberation and anarchism, is an intersectional transformative holistic theory-to-action activist led based movement and field of study to unapologetically examine, explain, be in solidarity with, and be part of radical and revolutionary actions, theories, groups and movements for total liberation and to dismantle all systems of domination and oppression, in hopes for a just, equitable, inclusive, and peaceful world. (Institute for Critical Animal Studies, 2017)

Furthermore, CAS scholar-activists published in 2007 the ten principles of critical animal studies (Best, Nocella, Kahn, Kemmerer, & Gigliotti, 2007), which they created together as members of ICAS to articulate the principles of CAS. To clarify CAS, we provide an explanation of each principle. The first principle dictates that we pursue interdisciplinary collaborative writing and research in a comprehensive manner that includes perspectives typically ignored by animal studies such as political economy. Thus, we collaborate with each other for organizing and activism such as books, conferences, rallies, protests, die-ins, civil disobedience, podcasts, blogs, social media, and writing essays and book chapters. The next principle encompasses rejecting pseudo-objective academic analysis by explicitly clarifying its normative values and political commitments, such that there are no positivist illusions whatsoever that theory is disinterested or writing and research is nonpolitical. In other words, we own and articulate one's subjectivity; locate and take ownership of one's domination, supremacy, and privilege and what one is doing to challenge it. This can occur at the beginning of a presentation, lecture, panel discussion, roundtable, workshops, teach-in, rally, protest, book chapter, book, essay, or conference to explain one's socio-political and economic status and experiences. The third principle mandates that we avoid eschewing narrow academic viewpoints and the debilitating theory-for-theory's sake position in order to link theory to practice, analysis to politics, and the academy to the community. We actively work to dismantle and disassociate one's self, movement and group from academia, academics, academies, and the academic industrial complex as they institutionalize and detach from social movements because they are part of the dominating schooling system and a bureaucracy. Rather, we are scholar-activists who engage daily in local communities and radical revolutionary activism, which informs our scholarship and in return our scholarship informs our activism and aids the movement.

The fourth CAS principle advances a holistic understanding of the commonality of oppressions, such that speciesism, sexism, racism, ableism, statism, classism, militarism and other hierarchical ideologies and institutions are viewed as parts of a larger, interlocking, global system of domination. We provide ample support for community circles and transformative justice on addressing conflict and see conflict as an opportunity to learn about others, oneself, and socio-political and economic issues, rather than a negative situation. Furthermore, our fifth directive rejects apolitical, conservative, and liberal positions to advance an anti-Capitalist and, more generally, a radical anti-hierarchical politics. This orientation seeks to dismantle all structures of exploitation, domination, oppression, torture, killing, and power for decentralizing and democratizing society at all levels and on a global basis. Our supporters advocate for anarchism and is an anarchist beyond simply lifestyle, but for socio-political and economic reasons. The sixth decree rejects reformist, single-issue, nation-based, legislative, strictly animal interest politics for alliance politics and solidarity with other struggles against oppression and hierarchy. We support and engage through activism intersectionality by being in solidarity and alliances with other movements. We understand that people, groups, and communities have multiple invisible and visible identites stemming from socio-political and economics constructions. The seventh delegation champions a politics of total liberation which grasps the need for, and the inseparability of, human, nonhuman animal, and Earth liberation and freedom for all in one comprehensive, though diverse, struggle; to quote Martin Luther King Jr.: "Injustice anywhere is a threat to justice everywhere." To participate in total liberation, we engage in other revolutionary radical activism and movements and do not identify as one type of activist over another or an activist promoting a particular issue over another or at other movement events.

The eigth principle of CAS requires deconstructing the socially constructed binary oppositions between human and nonhuman animals, a move basic to mainstream animal studies, but also looks to illuminate related dichotomies between culture and nature, civilization and wilderness and other dominator hierarchies to emphasize the historical boundaries placed upon humanity, nonhuman animals, cultural/political norms, and the liberation of nature as part of a transformative project that seeks to transcend these limits towards greater freedom, peace, and ecological harmony. The ninth principle requires openly examining controversial radical politics and strategies used in all kinds of social justice movements, such as those that involve economic sabotage from boycotts to direct action toward the goal of peace. This includes supporting, by any means necessary, revolutionary radical action that breaks the law such the aboveground civil disobedience such as home demos and sit-ins, underground groups such as the Animal Liberation Front, and armed struggle such as the Zapatistas and the former Black Panther Party. And finally the, tenth principle of CAS seeks to create openings for constructive critical dialogue on issues relevant to CAS across a wide-range of academic groups; citizens and grassroots activists; the staffs of policy and social service organizations; and people in private, public, and nonprofit sectors. Through—and only through—new paradigms of ecopedagogy, bridge-building with other social movements, and a solidarity-based alliance politics, is it possible to build the new forms of consciousness, knowledge, social institutions that are necessary to dissolve the hierarchical society that has enslaved this planet for the last ten thousand years. These principles aid in explaining and defining CAS and serve as strong guidelines for CAS scholar-activists. As educators, we want our students and newcomers to ICAS to clearly understand these points (ICAS, 2017).

Combating Ableism & Racism

We believe the two fastest growing issues within the intersectional movement, and field of CAS are challenging racism and ableism in connection with the liberation of animals. We believe that all CAS scholars ought to be fully committed to the intersectional complexities of oppression and work toward total liberation. Our message is that none of us can speak for other species, People of Color, or persons that identify as having a disability or as being perceived as disabled. Nor can we do adequate justice to any perspective other than that of four privileged scholar-activists who admit they benefit from human white-supremacy (Anthony and Johnny also benefiting as well from being male identifying)—and relatively temporarily able-bodied. Rather we are committed to not exploiting those privileges and we work each day to not only address them but both do everything we can to alleviate and eliminate the inequity of those privileges.

As CAS does, eco-ability and critical disability scholars focus on the interconnected ways in which discourses of modernity such as Cartesian dualism impacts perceptions of (dis)ability (Nocella II, Bentley, & Duncan, 2012). Nocella, Bentley, and Duncan (2012), emphasizing the importance of connecting ableism and speciesism as "social constructions interwoven into society, promoting civilization, normalcy, and intellectualism grounded in modernity" (p. 8), defines Eco-ability as:

> The theory that nature, nonhuman animals, and people with disabilities promote collaboration, not competition; interdependency, not independence; and respect for difference and diversity, not sameness and normalcy. (p. 9)

The Eco-Ability movement—which intersects with critical disability studies and CAS—focuses on how dominant assumptions of Western industrial culture have created the very socio-cultural conditions for ableist conceptions of personhood to exist as a constructed "normalcy." This hinges on a particular language and cultural practices to maintain a system of exploitation, necessitating a closer look at anthropocentrism—the belief system that situates humans at the center of everything and hierarchically superior to all Otherized beings. CAS scholars interrogate the ideological manifestation of anthropocentrism in relationship to humanist habits of culture that emerge in connection with an ontology of being rooted in Western philosophy and science (Nocella II et al., 2014). Collings (2012) explains:

> While anthropocentrism has led to the grim reality of widespread forest clearing, fish trawling, pollution and war, combined with the deadly practice of eugenics, this ideology has produced racial segregation, mass murder, and genocide and has led to deadly experiments on billions of human and nonhuman beings. (pp. 92–93)

Further, Collings asserts that "while disability scholars have argued that ethics of the body must begin with the unstable category of *disability*" she suggests that "the category of *animal* must also be considered as an inherent part of the equation" (p. 93). Collings states: "Those viewed as *disabled* and those viewed as animal have both been figured as strange and are devalued due to perceived biological inferiority" (p. 93).

CAS and eco-ability scholarship overlap in that they agree the neoliberalized perception of self in relationship to dominant social constructions of normal is a manifestation of anthropocentric discourses and thus can be understood and resisted through a process detailed in this paper. For those of us disciplined by "normalized" assumptions of human superiority and privileged by dominant definitions of ability, the challenge to address the complex and inextricable relationship between theory and action also becomes a challenge of doing so in accessible ways. In other words, while CAS seeks to interrupt dominant assumptions and privileges among academics and activists, it also requires a humble departure from a language of exclusion to practices that are accessible and inclusive of all. The question then is not: How do we do this through a CAS framework as outlined by the principles mentioned above? Rather, we ask: How might we continue to align with CAS principles while tending to the sensitive matter of ensuring that we work in unbounded ways to be accessible to all.

Understanding Ableism: Toward Eco-Ability and Anti-Ableism in CAS

Similar to the roots of racism, ableism emerged out of the ideology of normalcy that divides the world into a socially constructed binary of abnormal vs. normal. The normal are civilized, white, able-bodied, Christian, wealthy, domestic, formally educated, heterosexual, men; the abnormal are savage, primitive, interdependent, disabled, economically disadvantaged, non-educated, People of Color, women, non-Christian, animalistic, wild, and queer. Furthermore, non-human animals are routinely disabled by the conditions of factory farming, captivity in zoos and other entertainment industries, and animal testing. Industrially farmed animals live in such unnatural and horrendously filthy conditions that disabilities have become a common, if not inevitable, outcome.

The first phase of marginalizing a group into the abnormal category is by stigmatizing them. Western culture is replete with comments meant to demean humans through comparison to nonhuman animals: "you are such a pig," "you are acting like an animal," "stop acting like a bitch," "he's a dog," or "you are as fat as a cow." Similarly, people with disabilities are stigmatized and marginalized by comments such as: "you are retarded," suggesting a person is not intelligent; "you are a freak," suggesting a person has uncommon sexual behaviors or simply acts outside the norm; "why are you acting so lame?" suggesting a person is annoying or uncool; and "you are acting crazy," suggesting a person is not in control of their actions (Snyder & Mitchell, 2006). The animal advocacy movement is not free from such ableist terminology. Meat eaters are called "crazy," "stupid," "dumb," "idiotic," or "retarded." We all have overheard such conversations, and when we question the speaker's word choice, the response is often defensive rather than reflective.

People who challenge the norm and go against the grain of conventional societal messages regarding non/humans are marginalized alongside people with disabilities and other stigmatized populations. For instance, Diane Beers (2006) writes in, *For the Prevention of Cruelty: The History and Legacy of Animal Rights Activism in the United States,* "Several late nineteenth-century physicians concocted a diagnosable form of mental illness to explain an over concern for animal welfare. Sadly, they pronounced, that animal activists were misguided souls that suffered from 'zoophile psychosis'" (p. 309). As Beers describes, "zoophile psychosis" was mostly used to diagnose women "particularly susceptible to the malady." Since the early animal advocacy movement in the U.S. was primarily comprised of (white) women, such charges upheld subjugation of women, people with disabilities, and nonhuman animals alike. The label "zoophile psychosis" demeaned those who have mental illness and the women falsely diagnosed, as well as detracted from animal liberation efforts (Beers, 2006).

Similarly, when anti-oppression activists are brave enough to think critically and act against injustice, they are portrayed in the media as abnormal or "freaks." Activists and vegans who oppose consuming animal products are characterized in the media as overly zealous, human haters, spacey and neurotic, even terrorists. Furthermore, living in a society saturated with ableist and speciesist media, well-intentioned activists and advocates often misuse language, metaphor, and representation, inadvertently reproducing oppression and privileging one group at the expense of others. Even within the animal advocacy movement, many, from queer/trans scholar-activists to anarcho-ALF supporters, use ableist language and strategies. On blogs and Facebook, activists call animal abusers—and each other—"idiots," "blind to the truth," "psychotic," etc. Another example is that of Rory Freedman and Kim Barouin, authors of *Skinny Bitch* (2010), who in marketing their book write: "Stop being a moron and start getting skinny." However, using these outdated medical terms without any self-reflection suggests that those individuals are being reactionary and, albeit unintentionally, oppressive. Lacking any expertise in medicine, psychology, or psychiatry, they borrow terminology in a futile attempt to fight oppression from those industries that have aided in the construction of normalcy. In other words, they are trying to fight oppression with a form of abuse that they do not acknowledge. Academics, Facebookers, and bloggers are not the only ones using ableist language. At a fur protest recently Anthony heard two classic chants: "When animals are abused, what do you do? Stand up! Fight back!"; another chant was "Stop the murder! Stop the pain! Neiman Marcus is insane!" The first chant is ableist because of its lack of inclusion of those that are not able to physically stand.

The second chant is ableist because of use of the term "insane," which stigmatizes those with mental disabilities as being violent.

Additionally, some larger sized or "overweight" individuals may feel completely disenfranchised or even shamed for not being able to adhere to specific, and often arbitrarily set, vegan guidelines. When vegans proclaim a regimen of eating "healthiest" or "most sustainable" they overlook the fact that all bodies are different. Vegan diets, for example, are usually high in carbohydrates with protein sources that are high in starch such as beans, tofu, and quinoa. This may be fine for many people, but it's often not healthy for type 1 and type 2 diabetics, for whom excessive carbohydrates could mean a dangerous spike in blood glucose levels that lead to limb numbness and vision issues. For someone with Crohn's condition, a diet high in fiber, fruit, and vegetables could potentially trigger a flare-up. The point is not that a vegan diet is wrong, but rather that food policing or shaming along with adopting the one-diet-fits-all mantra disregards the serious structural and attitudinal barriers that are exclusionary both in terms of racism and ableism.

Eco-ability is an emerging movement whose approach to dealing with these issues is to inspire greater collaboration. The movement combines disability studies, environmental studies, and CAS. These fields form a philosophical framework that reweaves the isolated strands of environmental, disability, and nonhuman animal activism into a more potent and resilient movement. This structure directly confronts fragmentation by focusing on how the shared principles, practices, and experiences of these movements can bring forth new possibilities for mobilization, inclusion, and justice. Founded in 2011, eco-ability was outlined in *Earth, Animal, and Disability Liberation: The Rise of the Eco-ability Movement* (Nocella II et al., 2012). This book aided in the establishment of the Eco-ability Collective founded in that same year to organize events and publications. In 2015, the Eco-ability Collective and ICAS held the 3rd Annual Eco-ability Conference. Today, eco-ability reaches a global audience with two journal issues dedicated to the topic, three annual conferences, and many events centered on the theme, and two books are coming out in 2017. The central topics in eco-ability are: ableism in the environmental and animal advocacy movements; challenging animal use and testing for those with disabilities; critically examining the objectification and exploitation of animals with disabilities; challenging the concept of normalcy and how it is practiced within the environmental and animal advocacy movements; how systems of domination have fostered ableism, specicsism, and ecocide; and promoting how disability, uniqueness, and interdependency is supported and embraced by nonhuman animals and the natural world.

Anthony has created eight values of eco-ability: (1) difference and diversity, (2) holistic transformation through dialogue and education, (3) inclusive social justice and a total liberation movement, (4) intersectional, solidarity, and alliance politics, (5) being against all forms of oppression and domination, (6) engagement in critical theory and practice, (7) techno-digital justice, and (8) a collaborative and interdependent web of life.

Challenging Racism within CAS

Eco-ability draws from collaboratively diverse fronts to radically transform, respond to, and reframe dominant systems that undermine social justice and sustainability. Anti-racist politics are crucial in this framework to fight against normalcy and Western Eurocentric culture that enacts violence every day. Racism and colonialism are entrenched within the animal advocacy movement. Since animal advocacy is a Western philosophy emerging out of white society, one could argue it is rooted in both. Furthermore, colonialism and racism detached themselves from nature and are positioned in opposition to nature, constructing a binary of civilized versus savage and domestic versus wild. Colonialism and racism within the animal rights movement of today can include tokenizing People of Color, disproportionately focusing on criminalizing People of Color as the primary culprits of animal abuse, ignoring People of Color who are involved in the movement, and neglecting the impact that food insecurity can have on people's ability to live a vegan way of life.

People of Color have been tokenized in the animal rights movement in several ways. Unfortunately, such tokenizing of People of Color is nothing new as Women of Color have been exoticized within the movement through advertisements, outreach materials, social media images, and objectification practices. Thus, reenacting violence or co-opting the abuse experienced by any marginalized group or "suffering for the cause," is an unacceptable organizing stunt that will not lead to eradicating injustice and powerlessness. Co-opting positions of disempowerment is fraught with political and social implications that imply negative associations, stereotypes, and behavioral expectations that can take an immense toll on one's sense of pride and self-esteem. Furthermore, the process of co-opting can also have damaging effects on other organizing members who believe they are being good allies, doing the right thing by "raising consciousness," acting in an "inclusive" manner, and bringing more "diversity" to Animal Rights organizing by tokenizing such individuals and experiences.

Unfortunately, the media is guilty of framing television news broadcasts and newspaper stories about illegal animal entertainment as criminalizing People of Color and using racist and colonial systems such as the criminal justice system. For instance, an argument from those within the Animal Rights movement is that Michael Vick is wealthy, famous, Man of Color, ran an illegal dog fighting ring and abused canines. As one might expect, the law and race are inherently connected here when considering this argument. While there is no doubt that Vick broke the law, what he did is comparable to what other people of color and white people do when they attend legal animal performance such as bull riding, zoos, rodeos, and marine aquariums for family fun and entertainment. Television commercials often present animal entertainment opportunities with smiling white parents and their excited white children. But, we rarely watch on the evening news issues of wealthy white folks who also partake in legal and illegal abuse of animals for entertainment and profit purposes. Thus, much of what the public comes to understand as animal abuse undergoes specific racist framing that implicates not only People of Color but also other forms of animal entertainment in the United States such as cockfighting associated with Latino communities.

Another issue of importance within these movements is not promoting, supporting, or citing People of Color because it is assumed there are no People of Color in the animal advocacy or veganism movement. One only need cite the many Soul Vegetarian restaurants that have been in existence since the 1980s to understand that many People of Color have been involved with veganism for a long time, whether as a personal choice or political one. It is absurd to assume that People of Color do not care about animal rights, as there are those who do not partake in eating animals based on ethical grounds, both in Western and non-Western cultures. For instance, there are traditions from Chinese and Indian cultures, dating back thousands of years that promote compassion for non-human lives and the environment. Despite these traditions, some of the most aggressive non/human animal liberation campaigns target Asian cultures and politics. Consider the dolphin slaughter in Taiji, Indonesian policy towards slaughtering orangutans, the cat and dog meat industry in China, or the fur trades across many cultures in Asia. These campaigns seem to suggest that all people from Asian cultures are not interested in animal liberation. Labeling everyone associated with these nations as being anti-animal rights is racist. Whether one is presently or historically tied to a culture that may or may not benefit from animal exploitation, one cannot generalize that all populations engage in these problematic behaviors and beliefs.

We must recognize that there are People of Color in the animal rights movement, however, it may be difficult to acknowledge their contributions when there is so much focus on white perspectives. White people who may not have come to terms with their own racial privilege may have difficulty being inclusive on account of their own fears or prejudices. One common and problematic assumption made often by white scholar-activists is their apprehension to, or avoidance of, inviting People of Color to join their organizing. In this case, it's often that the white scholar-activist perceived that focusing on the rights of animals was privileged position. While on one hand these white scholar-activists aware of this are not entirely incorrect, it often can be a position of privilege. In fact, if one is organizing for animal rights without acknowledging and supporting the importance of the material suffering of their activist friends at the hand of the systemic oppressions of Western Industrial society (for example heteronormative-ableist-patriarchal and racist structures) then the white scholar activist is missing the importance of the ways that these injustices are deeply entangled and thus require we fight them on all fronts. Furthermore, no one should define when, how, and where a Person of Color should enter the movement or constrain their participation to conform to whites' expectations. Adherence to this reinforces white supremacy and paternalistic thinking by supporting the notion that only white people know what is best for People of Color. In the last decade, more People of Color have joined the cause, and many of them are challenging racism within the movement and from a decolonial perspective.

Some activists have gone so far as to accuse People of Color of not caring about animals because they are not vegan, rather than understand that issues of class, culture, food justice, and environmental justice may influence their ability to be vegan. For instance, Amber has witnessed vegans attacking People of Color's notion of animal rich "soul food" rather than try to understand its legacy within a cultural context. Soul food for many represents a sense of belonging, community, demonstrating one's sense of cultural pride. People of Color are not the only ones to indulge in animal laden meals as a part of tradition or culture, as many people equate consuming animal products with abundance. Thus, in the largely white-centered animal rights and vegan movements in America today, issues that impact People of Color like racism, classism, and heritage go largely ignored. This omission is unsurprising given that most representations of veganism are predominantly white-centric, and the activism used prioritizes theories, approaches, and practices created by white people and their perspectives, which have excluded People of Color. Additionally, there is very little to attract People of Color to animal rights, CAS, or veganism activism and scholarship. Furthermore, many individuals would perhaps choose to be vegetarian or vegan, if it weren't for the fact they live in low-income areas with minimal food choices and are subject to a government that subsidizes and promotes animal laden, fat-heavy diets versus ones with vegetables and fruits. CAS scholars are aware of the racial and class privilege many white vegans benefit from when making vegan dietary choices in the midst of expensive health food stores, farmer's markets, and accessible grocery stores in general. Whether it is the ability to buy and afford produce or to possess the free time to prepare vegan meals, CAS scholars advocate against the institutional and environmental racism that segregates People of Color into neighborhoods that lack grocery stores, farmer's markets, and the ability to harvest gardens.

Many white vegan chefs are trying to "exoticize" vegan cooking to make it more "ethnic" or make veganism stem from a position of "other." Equating veganism with exotic is not desirable if we seek to emancipate everyone and all from the damaging clutches of colonialism and imperialism. Case in point, the cookbook *Skinny Bitch in the Kitch* (2007) suggests that many "ethnic" or international cuisines are already vegan, so white people can pretend to be cooler and more worldly if they just make one of the global goodies listed in the book such as, falafel, pad thai, or veggie enchiladas. By making these foods exotic or emphasizing their ethnic nature implies they are there to be mastered, conquered, or accommodate the white Western desire to experience other cultures, without, of course, actually interacting with "the other."

CAS and Digital Activism/Justice

Early CAS scholarship has primarily focused on bridging the academy with the street, using an intersectional, anti-capitalist framework. In addition to these important links, CAS scholar-activists can also interrogate the digital realm as an extension of knowledge production and re-production. Earlier in this chapter, Anthony and Amber alluded to the ways in which social media can provide a space for both positive, transformational work, but simultaneously reproduce and magnify racist and ableist messages. The examination of social media platforms is of relevance to CAS scholars because understanding the narratives that are perpetuated and distributed on a massive scale provides insight into what is working effectively (or what needs to be addressed) in our movement.

Digital activism, through such online platforms as Instagram, Facebook, YouTube, and Twitter has worked effectively as a tool for uniting activists, mobilizing activists, and spreading awareness about important issues. Our collaboration as authors in this chapter, for instance, was made possible through our digital connections. As well, we use social media to augment the reach and publicity of grassroots activism. As evidenced by the Black Lives Matter movement, and #MMIW to investigate Canada's missing and murdered Indigenous women, social media can be used on a large scale to demand that injustices cannot be ignored.

The vegan movement has a solid presence in online domains, but the digitizing of activism (especially single-issue activism) means that a great deal of work remains for CAS scholar-activists. On a recent Facebook post, a vegan posted a photo comparing images of slavery to factory farming. When Meneka commented about the problematic nature of these images, she was told multiple times that she was wrong, and at one point was even told that her opinion was "not relevant," reinforcing the notion of public spaces as white spaces. Photographs of Black and Brown bodies are also used in vegan "poverty porn" to support the argument that grain used to feed non-humans could be used to eradicate world hunger. Aside from the logistical conundrum of why capitalist systems would continue to produce grain if demand for "food" animals (and therefore profits) no longer existed, these images promote the interests of veganism while ignoring the many complex food justice problems that exist for People of Color. It is also popular for vegan social media images to utilize the hashtag "cruelty free." This term positions vegans as highly privileged and either unaware of or indifferent to the human cruelties involved in capitalist systems of food production, to which vegan foods are not immune.

To make veganism an accessible and inclusive movement, those of us in the vegan community ought to discuss and work to address the complications that are tied to justice. The online assumptions that global veganism will resolve the world's problems, and that veganism is the end point of learning, and personal development should be a starting point for a stronger CAS perspective in online communities. CAS is and should continue to use digital platforms pedagogically to dismantle social power dynamics that are mirrored on social media. In addition to engaging in meaningful discussions about the intersections of veganism, racism, and ableism, CAS scholar-activists can work towards digitally reproducing scholarship and information to fit the "flavor" of social media. As an example, this may include infographics that are visually appealing and contain very little text, but continue to retain the integrity of good scholarship. By linking CAS principles with digital activism, as a companion to street activism, CAS can challenge the perpetuation of racist and ableist narratives in the online world.

Strategies to Fight Ableism and Racism

To challenge racism, colonialism and ableism within and outside of the animal advocacy movement, we must first take accountability and responsibility for the historical and modern theories and practices that are perpetrated therein. Next, we must genuinely, with no hidden agenda, listen to those with disabilities and People of Color and also become involved in their movements. Being involved, however, does not mean joining a cause to promote veganism or animal advocacy, but to listen to others' stories and to become involved in another cause. In working together, everyone must have an equal part in the learning and teaching of each other's movements and struggles. This pedagogical and organizational strategy is known as co-learning and can be summarized as follows: It refers to a mutual learning process exemplified by the phrase, "I am one of the teachers and one of the learners in this movement." It is collaborative; we create a community of cooperation, have conversations with centers not sides, and move away from competition and exclusion toward increased partnership.

In conclusion, one must be willing to become an ally, and that means being ready to be challenged and challenge others, rather than waiting for a person with disabilities or a Person of Color to address racism and ableism. Activists and scholars need to build an understanding of, and empathy for, the narratives of others in the group—not only the positions or opinions expressed, but also the underlying assumptions, values, needs and fears. In the process, they need to build a clearer understanding of their assumptions, values, needs and concerns, as well as their personal relationship to the issues being explored. We have demonstrated some strategies for becoming an effective ally in this essay. We have invited not only scholars and Activists of Color but also people with disabilities and those who support people with disabilities to expand upon CAS scholarship and Eco-ability theoretical frameworks. The authors of this essay have also taken personal and political accountability of their privilege and supremacy by reflecting on the real ways our identities and experiences are shaped by our particular social positioning. We have put forth our commitment and passion for social justice because we understand that some of our privileges provide us with social mobility and cultural capital often not afforded to other humans and non/humans alike. Part of our social consciousness is directly influenced by our willingness to be responsible for the direct and indirect ways we benefit from systems of oppression. Furthermore, we have shed light on those entities that perpetuate the tokenization, patronization, and appropriation of those who occupy statuses of non/white, non/human, disabled, and "othering" statuses to dismantle covert acts of oppression.

References

Beers, D. L. (2006). *For the prevention of cruelty: The history and legacy of animal rights activism in the United States.* Athens, OH: Swallow Press/Ohio University Press.

Best, S., Nocella II, A.J., Kahn, R., Kemmerer, L. & Gigliotti, T. (2007) Introducing Critical Animal Studies. ICAS. Retrieved from http://www.criticalanimalstudies.org/wp-content/uploads/2009/09/Introducing-Critical-Animal-Studies-2007.pdf

Collings, S. (2012). Transnational feminism and eco-ability: Transgressing the borders of normalcy and nation. In A. J. Nocella, J. K. C. Benty, & J. M. Duncan (Eds.), *Earth, animal, and disability liberation: The rise of the eco-ability movement* (pp. 91–107). New York, NY: Peter Lang Publishing.

David, M. B. (2014). *Through the 1950s, Africans and Native Americans were kept in zoos as exhibits.* Retrieved from http://politicalblindspot.com/through-the-1950s-africans-and-native-americans-were-kept-in-zoos-as-exhibits/

Freedman, R., & Barnouin, K. (2007). *Skinny bitch in the kitch: Kick-ass recipes for hungry girls who want to stop cooking crap (and start looking hot!).* Philadelphia, PA: Running Press.

Freedman, R., & Barnouin, K. (2010). *Skinny bitch: Ultimate everyday cookbook.* Philadelphia, PA: Running Press.

Institute for Critical Animal Studies (ICAS). (2017). "About." Retrieved from http://www.criticalanimalstudies.org/about/

Nocella II, A. J. (2014). Building an animal advocacy movement for racial and disability justice. In W. Tuttle (Ed.), *Circles of compassion: Essays connecting issues of justice.* Danvers, MA: Vegan Publishers.

Nocella II, A. J., Bentley, J. K. C., & Duncan, J. M. (Eds.). (2012). *Earth, animal, and disability liberation: The rise of the eco-ability movement.* New York, NY: Peter Lang Publishing.

Nocella II, A. J., Sorensen, J., Socha, K., & Matsuoka, A. (Eds.). (2014). *Defining critical animal studies: An intersectional social justice approach for liberation.* New York, NY: Peter Lang Publishing.

Snyder, L. & Mitchell, D. (2006). *Cultural locations of disability.* Chicago, IL: University of Chicago Press.

2. The Interdependency of Humans and Nature: A Plea for Ecopedagogy and Eco-ability Activism

Sarah R. Adams

The Split Between Humans and Nature

In our colonized and patriarchal society, we are often faced with many subconscious traumas that typically surface as negative psychological functioning. On top of that, we also live in a capitalistic world that feeds off of people's materialism, causing us to be massively consumed in personal gain; also known as being overly occupied with the ego. Society has been constructed in a way that makes us feel separate from anything larger than ourselves that does not involve money, particularly our planet. Being disconnected from the environment perpetuates the greatest illusion of separation, leaving us fluctuating between binaries. However, in the field of environmental psychology, it has been discovered that when an individual is submerged into nature and is forced be harmonious with it, there are positive psychological effects (Hawkins, Townsend, & Garst, 2016, p. 59). Environmental psychology is defined as a "discipline that studies the interplay between individuals and their built environment" (Steg, Van den Berg, & De Groot, 2012, p. 2). Nature as therapy, or ecotherapy, is a way of healing individuals with nature in mind. However, it is crucial to note the selfishness of ecotherapy because it is only viewed as a therapeutic technique that can benefit humans. Ecotherapy does not reciprocate care to the environment. Noting the positive effects of ecotherapy is only relevant because, unfortunately, many people do not feel the need to change unless there are personal benefits involved. Proving the benefits nature has on humans is a means of encouraging people to incorporate nature-based learning, or ecopedagogy, into schools. In society there is an epidemic of nature deficiency, particularly the United States, and there is an urgent call for healing. Nature deficiency is referring to the consequences of the divorce between humans and nature. Littering, non-human animal and environment exploitation, non-human animal cruelty, and pollution epidemics are a few examples of the consequences of nature deficiency. Since ecotherapy can heal individuals, this concept should be expanded to ecopedagogy or nature-based learning in order to heal the collective and reciprocate care to the planet. In this chapter, I recount the lessons learned about the importance of eco-pedagogy in conjunction with eco-ability while protesting the construction of the Dakota Access pipeline at the Standing Rock Reservation in North Dakota. I stress the importance of eco-based learning in conjunction with eco-ability activism for creating public awareness in order to heal the collective issues that are harming the planet, people with disabilities, and non-human animals.

The Resistance in Standing Rock

I recently went to Standing Rock, North Dakota where, while participating in eco-ability activism, I learned my limitations and how I had to risk more, challenge my privileges and question internal supremacy toward others. With that being said, I strived not to participate in Native traditions as I am not Native, and did not want to disrespect or appropriate other cultures. Although I work in social justice, I do aid in perpetuating oppression by being ethnically white, having my own apartment with my own room, attending a public liberal arts college in a predominantly white town (Durango, Colorado), speaking English, and being able-bodied. Moreover, I am a yoga practitioner and instructor, which is not historically from my ethnic culture. However, I strive to challenge myself and others about cultural appropriation and commodification for understanding the difference between being part of a culture and appreciating and being in solidarity with that culture.

Standing Rock's resistance to the Dakota Access Pipeline is about protecting land and water from the petroleum and gas industry drilling and laying a pipeline that can cause mass pollution. Thousands of people from all over the world joined the Sioux in solidarity in order to protect Earth's resources from exploitation and to restore mindfulness towards sacred lands. Despite all of the mistreatment towards water protectors and the lack of media coverage, we organized and demonstrated with the intention of raising awareness of the Earth's interests, which ultimately rejects the cruel forces that perpetuate materialism in the society in which we live.

Several other undergraduate students and I camped in the Oceti Sakowin camp, where we had access to health care, schools for children, legal help, and other resources needed to sustain community life. We could sense that the entire community was established with a common interest to protect the water and the Earth from the dangerous effects of the oil and gas pipelines. The atmosphere was truly ecocentric in that the community radiated care and compassion toward everyone, and all were respected and treated fairly no matter age, race, sexuality, gender, ability, or ethnicity. I experienced an entirely different dimension of community than I had ever experienced before. It was truly a pleasure to be a part of it. I'm not suggesting that individuals should go hang out with Natives for some sense of spiritual revitalization, rather, the community experience at Standing Rock can explain the inherent value of the Earth. When the Earth is recognized and respected as the number one and primary provider for the entire ecosystem, humanity included, egoist consciousness dwindles, and a compassionate atmosphere flourishes. At Standing Rock, I learned that not only does the environment have a positive influence on individuals, but also positively impacts groups, and even more so when interdependency is recognized and care is reciprocated.

Call for Action

While at Standing Rock, I mindfully acknowledged that I was a guest of the community. For instance, I attended their prayers and ceremonies, and was profoundly moved by a parallel that existed between Native American spirituality and my practice of yoga. For example, a yogi/yogini practices meditation and sun salute at sunrise and sunset, just as the Native American Sioux practice ceremonies at those times. Like many of the Native Americans I met at Standing Rock who sought to express their sense of sacred in their lives that is formed between the connection between humans and nature, I do so through the practice of yoga. As a child, I always felt the Divine within me but struggled to express it through the Christian religions my mother tried to force me into joining. I remember feeling humiliated and out of place in church. Later in my life, I was introduced to the practice of yoga, and I was moved deeply by it. I began studying yoga philosophy until I was totally immersed in the practice and became a yoga devotee.

Among the many spiritual parallels between Native American spirituality and yoga that exist, there unfortunately is a negative one too. They have both been Westernized and commodified. Thus, cultural appropriation occurs when one superficially claims the identity of a yoga practitioner or yogi/yogini without being devoted to its spiritual practices. Similarly, it is also superficial and an act of cultural appropriation to wear Native American items or practice Native American rituals without understanding and being aligned with its meanings and intentions. Other culture's sacred practices are only to be embraced with humility, humbleness, and modesty. With this in mind, spiritual practices have the potential to be suitable for all people because they regard matters of the spirit, not the body.

Through yoga, I have become spiritually fulfilled because I've learned how to meditate and discover truths within myself, which is eternally fruitful. Practicing certain yoga techniques have also increased my awareness of Earth's intentions. In yoga, certain energy practices require non-possessiveness and connectedness with the Earth and body in order to obtain higher levels of awareness. This makes yoga practitioners ideal candidates for furthering the eco-ability movement due to their respect of and humility for the planet. Amidst the chaos that I often witness as a sociologist and activist who has participated in direct action against hate, racism, fascism, bigotry, and white supremacy, spiritual yoga has taught me how to stay grounded and at peace. In addition to protesting the Dakota Access Pipeline on the front lines, I have also protested against sexism and gender inequality. I am on the front lines against social inequality because I have witnessed the differential treatment afforded to me versus my peers based on social identity differences. For instance, when once taking part in a direct action with a friend, we were reprimanded by authorities for writing positive messages on a sidewalk in a park. My friend, who is Black, was harassed and threatened with jail time while I was set free without charges. Furthermore, I put myself on the front lines because I could see the torment my disabled peers experienced in high school. I put myself on the front lines because my brother, who is diagnosed with severe ADHD and paranoid schizophrenia, suffers only because he feels like a menace to society despite his many talents. Most importantly, I put myself on the front lines because I am an empath feeling the Earth suffering as her resources and creatures are continuously exploited.

Reflecting back to my time in Standing Rock, I remember a Lakota elder saying that the Earth teaches us everything we need to know. The planets nature teaches us compassion and interdependence towards all living things. Despite this organic perception, civilization has perpetuated a binary between humans and nature that is causing a massive amount of disparities (Nocella, 2012, p. 5). It is necessary for humans to awaken to the needs of our planet so that harmony[1] and balance can be restored. This philosophy toward nature

---

1. When using harmony and/or harmonious, it is meant to be defined as living in balance and recognizing interdependence.

is very similar to the foundations of eco-ability, a theory that was realized by Dr. Anthony J. Nocella. Nocella defines eco-ability as a "theory that nature, non-human animals, and people with disabilities promote collaboration, not competition; interdependency, not interdependence; and respect for difference and diversity, not sameness and normalcy" (Nocella, 2012, p. 9). Similar to the way in which Native American philosophies toward nature have been suppressed, eco-ability activism is not mainstream in our society because its ideological underpinnings and methods for change have been deemed inferior by Westernization. However, now more than ever, there is an urgent call for healing from our planet because environmental and social catastrophes are escalating.

Environment's One-on-One Care

Keeping in mind that systemic change can begin at the individual level, ecotherapy holds much promise for using nature as a means for healing individuals. Ecotherapy is a recreational therapeutic approach that merges individuals into the environment in order to "draw out the strengths of participants to promote therapeutic and continued development despite … health conditions and functional limitations" (Hawkins et al., 2016, p. 58). Ecotherapy includes many different activities and interventions to promote healing such as outdoor adventures, camping in groups, engaging cognitively with nature to discover symbolic thinking about the environment, and exploring nature with a therapist (Hawkins et al., 2016, p. 63). Acknowledging that each patient has differing and complex needs, nature's expansiveness can provide for those needs and then some. This enables the patient to participate in a nature-based intervention that is suitable to their individual needs (Hawkins et al., 2016, p. 62).

Unlike traditional therapy that expects a patient to be open with a complete stranger and potentially take medications to cope with mental issues, ecotherapy stresses connecting on various levels with inanimate and animate beings besides the self through holistic means. One study demonstrates the power that nature-based therapy has had for military service members. Analyzing military service members is significant because often they experience extreme post-traumatic stress, physical injuries, and disability labeling. The disability labeling that military service members are often subject to upon their return home from service adds to the societal notion that people with disabilities are faulty or undesirable. Being considered undesirable has negative effects on the psyche because it leaves one feeling ostracized and unworthy of being. One example of the marginalization of disabled people is the abundant use of ableist language in today's society (Nocella, 2012, p. 9). Using words like "crazy" or "freak" to shame someone is suggesting that people with mental disabilities are also shameful to society (Nocella, 2012, p. 9). Despite this, we see that ecotherapy still offered significant healing for military service members because they were able to resolve social, identity, mental, and spiritual disparities. Thus, military members, especially those with disabilities are likely in great need for support and therapy, giving further proof that ecotherapy should be given to those seeking assistance. Additionally, military members also show substantial dropout rates when undergoing traditional therapy (Hawkins et al., 2016, p. 58). Since many military service members have clearly been unsuccessful in traditional therapy because of their conditions, it is significant to analyze their response to nature-based therapy because it reveals the legitimate healing power that ecotherapy offers.

The outcomes for the military service members in ecotherapy interventions indicated that nature helps heal despite affliction or disability. Positive outcomes included "improvements in social, cognitive, and spiritual domains, as well as outcomes pertaining to identity, purpose, and overall recovery from life changes" (Hawkins et al., 2016, p. 59). Emphasis should be placed on these particular improvements because there is a link between them and spirituality, mindfulness, and community building. Moreover, it is apparent that connecting to the environment not only helps psychologically and physically, but also collectively because patients feel a revitalized sense of belonging within their community (Hawkins et al., 2016, p. 60). In a society that often criticizes people with disabilities, a revitalized sense of community is significant to note. The Earth appears to be directly related to the health of our species.

The inclusion of this analysis is to serve as evidence of the healing power that the Earth possesses for our species. Unfortunately, not all ecotherapy is collaborative which defeats the message of the eco-ability movement. Although ecotherapy has proven to revitalize patients understanding of connectedness and sense of community, it is still exploitative to the environment if care is not reciprocated. As long as ecotherapy is one sided it will not promote eco-ability. The ideas and techniques of ecotherapy do, however, have the potential to translate into ecopedagogy which could foster eco-ability activism in future generations. If it was mandatory for tenants of ecotherapy to reciprocate care to the environment, eco-ability activism would be the ideal response. Even if patients of ecotherapy had never been previously interested in conserving the Earth or nature, it is evident that they finish their interventions with a new and profound sense of interconnectedness. This new state of awareness could potentially foster a group of eco-ability activists who return care and solidarity to the Earth because nature helped them address their issues.

Collective Despair

Living in a society that is based on capitalism, it is no surprise that there is a disconnection from nature. A capitalistic system perpetuates greed, separating people from interconnectedness, and when we take too much for ourselves, we take from someone else. The "someone else" is typically the larger ecosystem which is comprised of species and nature. This disconnection has also perpetuated social afflictions within the human race such as marginalization of certain groups. Nocella explains that "[i]n Western civilization, the marginalization of those who are different was first fostered and reinforced by the concept of civilization and its divide between nature and humans" (Nocella, 2012, p. 6). There has been a failure to recognize that "humans as a species are a part of the 'animal kingdom' and nature, rather than separate and dominant" (Nocella, 2012, p. 5). The perception of being dominant over nature has led to greed, capitalistic mentality, and egocentrism. Ian E. Smith explains in an eco-ability conference that "civilization itself acts as a disabling force" and it "allows us to not care for others who may need assistance." This is blatantly obvious when observing the exploitation of the Earth's resources, deforestation, climate change, environmental terrorism, factory farming, animal cruelty, and many other issues that are leaving our planet in distress (Kahn, 2010, p. 3).

Similar to the stigmatization that disabled people experience, nonhuman animals are subject to oppression as well, because "nonhumans and people with disabilities share much in common..." (Basas, 2012, p. 194). Using speciesist language, similar to ableist shaming language, such as "you're such a dog" or "you're a pig" to shame others, suggests that animals are undesirable because it is being compared to behavior that has been disapproved by the speaker (Nocella, 2012, p. 9). To add on to the blatant cruelty towards animals, dominant Western language continues to humiliate them.

The tendency to overconsume continues to plague our species and is one of the major forces blocking our ability to be interdependent with each other within the ecosystem. In the article "The Human Glance, the Experience of Environmental Distress and the Affordance of Nature," it is stated that "humanity is using 50% more resources than Earth can provide" (Blok, 2016, p. 926). We overconsume products, nonhuman animals, and each other through exploitation in various settings. Take for example, the exploitation of animals trapped in factory farming and slaughterhouses. In factory farms, the actions performed on nonhuman animals such as cutting chick's beaks so they won't peck each other due to overcrowding suggests that the humans responsible for such cruelty have no empathy towards other forms of life. The perpetrators clearly have been led to believe they are separate and superior to nonhuman animals (Bentley, 2012, p. 33). Furthermore, the laborers who work in factory farming and slaughterhouses are often subjected to subpar working conditions, poor wages, instability, and illness. Besides, it is no coincidence that the exploitation of animals and resulting byproducts of factory farms and slaughterhouses have become one of the leading causes of climate change. This is one of the clearest examples of interconnectivity and interdependence. As long as humans feel separate from the environment, we will continue to behave in a harmful way against the planet, which affects all life.

Nonhuman animals are considered property by the mainstream collective, and not too long ago (one hundred years), so were people with disabilities (Basas, 2012, p. 194). They were used as "property to explore and exploit for labor and use and burdens when they seem no longer productive" (Basas, 2012, p. 194). This connection is another reason why eco-ability activism is crucial for social progression because as long as humans are treated as objects to be exploited for personal gain, nonhuman animals will be too. Eco-ability is a movement that demands the abolition of cruel forces such as civilization, capitalism, and colonialism that perpetuate the disparities that have arisen from nature deficiency.

The Root of Nature Deficiency

In a book titled "A New Earth: Awakening your Life Purpose," the author Eckhart Tolle dissects the ego and examines a collective dysfunction within our species. Tolle explains that

> [i]f the history of humanity were the clinical case of a single human being, the diagnoses would have to be: chronic paranoia, delusions, a pathological propensity to commit murder and acts of extreme violence, and cruelty against his perceived enemies. (Tolle, 2005, p. 12)

These collective tribulations are evident throughout the history of capitalistic colonizers. Tolle also explains:

> We need only to watch the daily news on television to realize that the madness has not abated, that is continuing into the twenty-first century. Another aspect of the collective dysfunction of the human mind is unprecedented violence that

> humans are inflicting on other life-forms and the planet itself—the destruction of oxygen-producing forests and other plant and animal life; ill treatment of animals in factory farms; and poisoning of rivers, oceans, and air. Driven by greed, ignorant of their connectedness to the whole, humans persist in behavior that, if continued unchecked, can only result in their own destruction. (Tolle, 2005, p. 11)

When Tolle explains that humans are motivated by greed, it is clear that the issues of humanity are rooted in egocentrism; being overly consumed in personal gain which causes separation of the self from the whole.

We must also note the effects that nature deficiency has on children because they are the future of our species. It would be preferable if a connection to nature was nurtured at an early age since nature-based interventions can provide revitalization regarding identity, social, mental, psychical, and spiritual realms. Unfortunately, many children today do not express connectedness with the Earth, which has a detrimental effect on development (Lindquist & Grimm, 2012, p. 130). Being sheltered from the environment could very well develop into negative cognitive functioning that could perpetuate negative environmental behavior.

Eco-ability and Ecopedagogy

The eco-ability movement requires healing that which divides our ability to be a collective. As a way to heal the collective dysfunction, we must go to the root of the issue—the illusion of separation and greed. Since ecotherapy nurtures community development, it is likely to help young people learn how to be harmonious with the environment and establish an organic awareness of connectivity. Through an awareness of connectedness to all life, pro-environmental behaviors become the natural way to behave and eco-ability activism is emboldened. This philosophy of learning was encouraged by the elders and camp leaders in the resistance camps in Standing Rock. The alert awareness of environmental rights that collectively existed and was encouraged in Standing Rock enlivened the community of water protectors.

Richard Kahn stated that

> if education for sustainable development is utilized strategically to advance the sort of radical ecopedagogy ... it could be a much-needed boost to social movements that are desperately attempting to respond to the cataclysmic challenges posed by unprecedented planetary ecocrisis. (Kahn, 2010, p. 3)

Kahn suggests that the integration of ecopedagogy into education will inspire activism regarding the ecocrisis—eco-ability—to be more prevalent. Unlike ecotherapy, ecopedagogy is not a single-focused technique that is solely for the benefit of humans. Ecopedagogy does reciprocate care to the environment because it boosts eco-ability activism. Ecopedagogy addresses the ecocrisis and prompts direct action to counteract it. The ecocrisis is urgent and any way to impede it should be welcomed by all educators.

Teachers play a crucial role in the implication of eco-ability in ecopedagogy "because they communicate strong and clear messages…" and their influence has a lasting affect on their student adolescents (Lindquist & Grimm, 2012, p. 136). In classrooms and educational settings, "[t]eachers project their emotions and beliefs, and students will behave in a manner that mirrors what they read" (Lindquist & Grimm, 2012, p. 136). It is evident that despite whatever circumstances a student may be experiencing at home, school generates strong social norms that students will adapt to regardless. If teachers project eco-ability onto the students through the utilization of ecopedagogy, we could begin to see generations that are directly involved in radical activism regarding the liberation of Earth, nonhuman animals, and people with disabilities that counteract the ecological crisis.

Although ecopedagogy is sometimes deemed as radical by some conservatives, nature-based learning is not an abstract idea. In fact, there have been many schools that have used this technique, and luckily, it has been studied and documented. One such study described by authors Ibrahim Acar and Julia Torquati, examine a school that uses techniques such as nature walks, group meetings in outdoor spaces, interactions with plants and animals, and many others to provide children a nature-based education. They suggest "children may learn concern, care, and empathy for living things through interactions and relationships with both human and nonhuman living things" (Acar & Torquati, 2015, p. 64). Cooperation, teamwork, and empathy are important qualities that manifest from a nature-based education; not greed, not isolation, not egocentrism. So from this observation, it is clear that nature can be used as a collective therapy if utilized correctly in schools. Schools are responsible for training humans on how to be harmonious with the world but without nature-based learning, this cannot be possible.

Mainstream education does not incorporate nature-based learning techniques into classrooms so it is no surprise that we continue to see an overwhelming disparity of nature deficiency. When children are allowed interactions with nature, prosocial behavior is likely to develop (Acar & Torquati, 2015, p. 63). Behaving respectfully toward the planet and one another while having positive community experiences encourages altruism, ecocentrism, and eco-ability. Ecopedagogy clearly promotes the eco-ability philosophy because and the ideology that is being encouraged "respects differences in abilities while promoting values appropriate to the stewardship of ecosystems" (Nocella, 2012, p. 5).

There is no better way to promote eco-ability than through ecopedagogy in educational based settings. It is also beneficial for parents and teachers because children in nature-based educational settings also prove to have reduced behavioral issues (Swank, Shin, Cabrita, Cheung, & Rivers, 2015, p. 442). Nature-based education or ecopedagogy is simply the larger picture and extension of ecotherapy, especially when considering the despair of our species and planet.

Conclusion: Requiting Nature's Hospitality

From analyzing the positive psychological, physical, spiritual outcomes of ecotherapy for military service members, it is evident that being immersed into nature is powerfully healing. Of course, it is unfortunate that the environment must be used as a therapeutic technique in the first place because one would hope that it is already an intimate part of the soul. However, it has been made clear that nature does not only serve as a means for healing; it also serves as a way to nurture community and a profound understanding of interconnectedness. We can predict to see a decrease in behavior that has been harmful to each other, nonhuman animals, and the Earth when the majority of humans in our world can revive their intimacy with the environment. An awareness that understands connectedness will be morally obligated to return care through radical eco-ability activism by speaking out on behalf of the Earth's interests.

It is now up to us to reciprocate care to the environment with eco-ability activism by dismantling the capitalist, colonialist, and civilization structures that have allowed negative environmental behaviors to prevail. Schools play the biggest role in this social movement because they foster the ideals and values that future generations will possess. Restoring balance for the planet and animals while demarginalizing people with disabilities is only possible if we begin to incorporate nature into our daily lives, especially education.

The resistance in Standing Rock is a manifestation of eco-ability activism that is a response to the ecocrisis and cruelty of corporate capitalism. While camping in Standing Rock I learned from residential water protectors that mainstream media coverage is limited and inadequate regarding the movement. It is up to the people to spread awareness through radical eco-ability activism because corporations are being allowed to take over land without consent of the people. Alas, we cannot expect people just to change their ways because we throw some facts their way. Healing must first take place. A shift in consciousness must occur on a mass scale, which could only be possible through the integration of critical ecopedagogy, sociology, and psychology. Environmental psychology offers the tangible proof of the healing power of nature; Sociology enables us to analyze collective issues and develop solutions; and lastly, ecopedagogy enforces the change. Through this integration and manifestation of ecopedagogy, eco-ability activism will rise. From recent political events that have taken place in the United States, it is clear that colonialist governments have structured civilizations in order to feed money-hungry capitalists who have no concern for life besides their own. Eco-ability activism demands concord between all living things. This will encourage self-sufficient communities that are not reliant on governments, but each other and the planet.

References

Acar, I., & Torquati, J. (2015). The power of nature: Developing prosocial behavior toward nature and peers through nature-based activities. *YC: Young Children, 70*(5), 62.

Basas, G. C. (2012). Private, public, or compassionate: Animal rights and disability rights laws. In Nocella, II J. A., Bentley, J. K. C., & Duncan, J. M. (Eds.), *Earth, animal, and disability liberation: The rise of the eco-ability movement* (pp. 187–202). New York, NY: Peter Lang Publishing.

Bentley, J. K. C. (2012). Human disabilities, nonhuman animals, and nature: Toxic constructs and transformative technologies. In Nocella, II A. J., Bentley, J. K. C., & Duncan, J. M. (Eds.), *Earth, animal, and disability liberation: The rise of the eco-ability movement* (pp. 22–37). New York, NY: Peter Lang Publishing.

Block, V. (2015). The human glance, the experience of environmental distress and the "affordance" of nature: Toward a phenomenology of the ecological crisis. *Journal of Agricultural and Environmental Ethics, 28*(5), 925–938.

Hawkins, B. L., Townsend J. A., & Garst, B. A. (2016). Nature-based recreational therapy for military service members: A strengths approach. *Therapeutic Recreation Journal, 50*(1), 55–74.

Kahn, R. (2010). *Critical pedagogy, ecoliteracy, & planetary crisis: The ecopedagogy movement* (Vol. 359). New York, NY: Peter Lang Publishing.

Nocella, II A. J. (2012). Defining eco-ability: Social justice and the intersectionality of disability, nonhuman animals, and ecology. In Nocella, II A. J., Bentley, J. K. C., & Duncan, J. M. (Eds.), *Earth, animal, and disability liberation: the rise of the eco-ability movement* (pp. 3–21). New York, NY: Peter Lang Publishing.

Steg, L., Van den Berg, A. E., & De Groot, J. I. (Eds.). (2012). *Environmental psychology: An introduction*. New York, NY: John Wiley & Sons.

Swank, J. M., Shin, S. M., Cabrita, C., Cheung, C., & Rivers, B. (2015). Initial investigation of nature-based, child centered play therapy: A single-case design. *Journal of Counseling and Development*, *93*(4), 440–450.

Tolle, E. (2005). *A new earth: Awakening to your life's purpose*. New York, NY: Dutton/Penguin Group.

3. From Collective Autism to Autistic Wildness

Daniel Salomon

I draw from my experiences being an Aspie, a published environmental writer and political activist to demonstrate why there is a conflict of interest between the neurodiversity and deep ecology movements and how this conflict could be resolved through interest-based conflict resolution.

I begin with a definition of deep ecology including delineating the branches of the deep ecology movement with their key arguments (ecocentrism, primitivism, ecofeminism and environmental justice) and impact on the environmental movement (preservation, humanities and climate). I will argue why deep ecology is a legitimate cause for neurodiversity (nonhuman oppression).

I than integrate Critical Environmental Studies with Critical Disability Studies.

I will reconstruct Zerzan's (2012, 2015, 2018) primitivist, anarchist critique of modern technology (hunters and gatherers argument), with psychology, environmental justice and neurodiversity, addressing concerns of exoticism, idealization and inaccessibility. I will accomplish this through Glendenning (1990, 1994, 2002, 2005) with psychology, McFague (1982, 2000a, 2000b, 2007) with environmental justice, and Prince-Hughes (2005) with neurodiversity.

I claim intersection between disability history and environmental history. Many modern technologies (such as roadmaps) used to create modern society (global imperialism) and the ideologies used to perpetuate (like Greek philosophy) are both the root causes of the planetary crisis and normalcy, a crip, neurodiverse variation on environmental historians Merchant (1990) and Hughes (1996).

A critique of the status quo is the greatest gift of deep ecology to neurodiversity and disability. Deep Ecology makes normal culturally specific to white society. This gives neurodiversity and disability a foothold for being able to question society.

I conclude with ways neurodiversity can advocate for nonhumans and deep ecology can incorporate neurodiversity. I accomplish this through identifying the mutual interest of neurodiversity and deep ecology needing to question the mechanistic foundations of Western civilization.

I call only for the elimination of technologies which thwart living organisms from surviving and flourishing, such as fast food and automobiles.

I contend using technology is compatible with critiquing the shadow sides of technology.

What Is Deep Ecology?

In the early 1970s there was a split in the environmental movement between mainline environmentalists (e.g., scientists) and radical environmentalists (e.g., philosophers) where radical environmentalists began to identify themselves as deep ecologists and labeled mainline environmentalists shallow ecologists.

Deep ecology was a response to the mainline environmental movement in the 1970s becoming increasingly elite, specialized, overly professional and compartmentalized, leading to weak versus strong responses to the impending socio-planetary crisis such as modest reforms versus radical-revolutionary changes.

Deep ecology as articulated by philosophers Arne Ness and George Session called for the Natural World to be respected and protected for its own sake versus merely for its usefulness to human beings. This was coupled with a call to preserve Earth's wildernesses and biodiversity, reduce human interference in Natural World, human population control, subsistence living, a more human scale political economic system, radical-revolutionary change at all levels of human society, putting theory into practice and practicing what you preach.

I will contend that the aspects of deep ecology which involve respecting that the Natural World exists for its own sake, the protection and preservation of wildernesses and biodiversity, some aspects of subsistence living, a more human scale political economic system, radical-revolutionary change, putting theory into practice and practicing what you preach is compatible with neurodiverse cultures, mad pride and disability justice.

Environmental justice concerns about deep ecology leaving in-tact individualism, inequality and imperialism was one of the reasons for further splits in the deep ecology movement into primitivism, ecofeminism and ecocentrism.

Primitivism felt the need to address how colonialism, alienation from the Natural World and each other and the socio-planetary crisis was also adversely impacting individual Westerners, calling for the ecological healing of individual Westerners through studying human evolution, dialoging with indigenous peoples around the world and engaging the Natural World and human community.

Ecofeminism was particularly concerned with how colonialism, alienation and the socio-planetary crisis was adversely impacting women (like the feminization of poverty in the Geographic South), how femininity and feminine Ideas of Nature have been systematically suppressed by patriarchy in the West (like privileging mechanism and compartmentalization over interconnectiveness and the ecological whole) and how patriarchy has also adversely ecologically impacted men (like the violent socialization of men into adulthood and the human costs of harmful technologies).

The Ecocentric branch of deep ecology which includes the animal movements and the wilderness preservation movements had concerns that environmentalist justice, primitivism and ecofeminism takes the focus off the Nonhuman World and back onto human beings, where environmentalism and animal liberation is reduced to an uncritical humanism which trivializes the reasons for protecting wilderness and animals for their own sake.

It is also important to point out that colonized humans in the Geographic South which also includes First Nations and women in the Geographic South, more than ever before are still disproportionately impacted by the most serious effects of the socio-planetary crisis because of the globalization of economic poverty, inequality and environmental devastation, combined with the increasing feminization of world poverty.

Attention to the geopolitical aspects of environmental inequality which links the globalization of human poverty in the Geographic South and human-induced environmental practices predominately in the Geographic North to the deterioration of the planet (like global climate change) is one of the most recent forms of the environmental justice argument popularized by religious leader Pope Francis.

Pope Francis has also included respect for disability dignity as part of his uniquely Roman Catholic human ecology. A vision which includes respecting the intrinsic value and the inherent worth, as well as the individuality, diversity and gifts of every disabled human around the world, from womb to grave, calling for all disabled humans to be included and accommodated, for artificial barriers to be eliminated, for all of us to be treated as individuals and for our gifts to be employed.

It is also important to point out that according to the United States International Council on Disabilities (USICD); disability is the world's largest minority. According to USICD, 57.8 million Americans have one or more disabilities, 5.5 million American veterans are people with disabilities, there are 1 billion people with disabilities around the world, 80% of people with disabilities live in developing countries, 1 in 4 of today's 20 year olds will be disabled before they retire and 80% of people with disabilities live in isolated rural areas.

Not only do environmentalists need the disabilities communities around the world as allies in the socio-planetary struggle, the disability community is definitely being unfairly affected and burdened by the socio-planetary crisis. We deserve to tell our own ecological autobiographies to the global human community, ourselves, speaking for ourselves, in our own words, from our own point-of-view.

I find ecocentrism the most persuasive because I empathize with the plight of Animals and Earth, because I see in the suffering of Animals and Earth, some of my own suffering and oppression as a neurodiverse human, where environmentalism and animal liberation then becomes a type of survivor mission for me. More importantly, Nature is the closest I have ever had to a childhood, lifelong friend, the only place where I felt safe and belonged, growing-up as an Aspie in a neurotypical, abelist, human society. Nature has been there for me, when humans have not. As a result, I have a sense of comradery, loyalty even solidarity with All Nature. This is the real reason why I am a life-long committed environmentalist and animal activist.

I have found primitivism, ecofeminism and environmental justice very helpful in preventing my human dignity from completely dissolving into All Nature through corroborating my Aspie experiences and maturing my eco-abilities, allowing me to reconnect with my human community, while preserving my unique Aspie ecological identity.

For example, primitivism has helped me reclaim my childhood experiences of ecstasy in Nature, preserving my sense of wonder, in the process, making it easier to more positively connect with other humans.

Ecofeminism, especially holistic cosmology (the world is a living organism), has validated my autistic propensity to personify inanimate objects, and inability to tune-out my environment which I was persecuted for as a child, youth and young adult.

Ecofeminism has also taught me respect for my own body, which inspired me to take better care of my own physical and mental well-being. All of this has helped me connect with movements addressing my neurodiverse self-understandings of Earth and the socio-planetary crisis (e.g., Critical Environmental Studies and Christian Environmentalism) which has led me to green communities which are equipped to utilize my eco-abilities (e.g., Portland Oregon and becoming a Roman Catholic). I am also now a citizen scientist, a lecturer and private tour guide for the Hoyt Arboretum in Portland, Oregon.

Neurodiversity is also now being addressed as a global climate change issue by the newly formed International Transformative Resilience Coalition (ITRC), a revitalization of the earlier ecopsychology movement, still another split of the deep ecology movement.

The ITRC is advocating for neurodiverse humans around the world as well as other oppressed minority groups, to educate both experts and the public alike, to the sobering reality that global climate change is creating the greatest mental health crisis in human history. Among other demands, the ITRC is calling for climate activists and policy makers to make provisions for us neurodiverse humanity when developing and implanting solutions to the global climate crisis including sensitivity to language about fear in environmental rhetoric.

Yet, we the neurodiverse, as well as disability communities around the world, still need to be playing a more active role in shaping, forming, implementing and realizing the goals of the socio-planetary agenda.

Putting Critical Disability Studies into Dialogue with Critical Environmental Studies

Critical Disability Studies must be in dialogue with Critical Environmental Studies. This is because Critical Environmental Studies is helping to put the logic in place for our deconstruction of normalcy and ableism through making what is normal culturally specific to white society, through defining normal as Eurocentrism, Imperialism, Modernism, Individualism, Classism and The Socio-Planetary Crisis. In other words, normal is the status quo, a status quo which is not working for anyone.

Critical Environmental Studies is also helping us reconstruct and recover neurodiverse cultures through linking neurodiverse intelligences, consciousness and abilities to the ways of Indigenous and traditional societies around the world.

In fact, we can now make a very strong Critical Environmental Studies argument that we, the neurodiverse have been colonized by the same forces which have colonized other minority groups and Planet Earth, helping to move autistic discourse from reductionism and deviance to human dignity even social justice.

Making Critical Environmental Studies Accessible to Critical Disability Studies

Zerzan (2012, 2015) offers a primitivist, anarchist critique of modern technology, claiming that the root cause of the socio-planetary crisis is a period in history, 10,000BC, when many societies around the world, especially in Eurasia, made the transition from being hunter/gatherers to farmer/herders to city-states. This shift in human-Earth relationships from mutuality to colonization inspired humanity to construct anti-ecological ideologies to justify imperialistic relationships with the Natural World and each other (e.g., speciesism). This put the logic in place during the European Enlightenment for today's anti-ecological practices (e.g., global habitat destruction, institutionalized animal cruelty and industrial pollution) causing our very serious socio-planetary crisis in the process.

The proposed solution than is for all humanity to go back to being hunter/gatherers. This is accomplished through studying the story of human evolution employing modern science and salvaging ecologically helpful elements of Western civilization. Learning the ways of colonized peoples around the world who are still living as hunter/gatherers like the Native Americans, coupled with directly engaging wild Nature unmediated through wilderness experiences and becoming hunter/gatherers (e.g., ethical hunting).

This is also accomplished through human population control, divesting from modern technologies, voluntary simplicity and community building through religious rituals and developing more human scale, sustainable and just ideologies, crafts, lifestyles and social institutions.

There is a sympathetic mainline environmentalist, environmental justice, animal liberationist critique of Zerzan's primitivist anarchy. There are three main objections!

The first objection is that anarchist primitivism can lead to exoticism which is a-historical at best, at-worst, can revitalize, even invent anti-ecological practices like ethical hunting, only to be left ethically-morally unquestioned.

The second objection is concerns about idealization of First Nation societies where various First Nation communities are then expected to live-up to these Western formulated ideals and when they do not, they are scapegoated with racism, leading to two types of paternalism:

One is reducing First Nation humans to moral patients versus moral agents. Seeing and treating First Nation peoples as morally innocent, ecological victims, incapable of making their own moral choices. Two is animalizing First Nation humanity as being childlike to be parented by the adults, we as Westerners, under the spell of the white man's burden narrative.

The final objection to anarchist primitivism is that the standard is so high and pure; it makes environmentalism inaccessible to most ordinary humans, so ordinary humans end-up doing nothing at all.

Some ecofeminists have attempted to revitalize anarchist primitivism through consciously integrating anarchist primitivism with Western ideals, developing what is now known as *communitarianism*. I have identified there different forms of communitarianism.

Trauma therapist/addiction specialist Glendenning has cross-pollinated anarchist primitivism with modern psychology through the archetype of the Wounded Healer. Addressing how the socio-planetary crisis has adversely impacted the individual psyches of Westerners. Coupled with how individual Westerners can heal from the adverse effects of colonization through being attentive to their environment and engaging in political activism cross-pollinated with conventional psychology and medicine.

The Wounded Healer is the universal human experience of a human with a disability developing the ability to heal others as a result. Glendenning contends that a disproportionate amount of Westerners have been disabled by modern technology and have developed the ability to heal others and help heal the planet through being able to have altered consciousnesses which allows us to "live more sanely and sustainability on this Earth" (Glendenning, 1994).

Glendenning's goal is not to cure us or make us normal, the opposite, defining healing as decolonialization (Glendenning, 2005), Glendenning is calling us to take back our identities and our lives from toxic narratives and technologies and to reconnect with all aspects of our society including our relationship with the Natural World. Glendenning contends "the personal is planetary, the planetary personal" (Glendenning, 1994, p. 162).

Glendenning's work implies that the social construction of disability (it's not our fault!) and disability culture (it's who we are!) are compatible with one another even through disability culture is not natural, because disability culture humanizes the technocratic aspects of modern life (Glendenning, 1994 p. 209).

Feminist Christian ecotheologian Sallie McFague cross-pollinates anarchist primitivism with environmental justice through linking consumerism in North America to anthropocentrism, environmental injustices in the

Geographic South and the socio-planetary crisis. Calling all North Americans to reduce overconsumption and become more communitarian, McFague also recognizes that many North Americans including disability and neurodiversity do not fit into conventional society and calls North American minorities to see our strengths of not fitting in as our wild space which we can use to critique the anti-ecological foundations of our society (*Life Abundant, a New Climate for Theology*).

In my books and papers, I identify my neurodiversity wild space as a challenge to anthropocentrism, speciesism, mechanization and compartmentalization.

This is because I personify inanimate objects and cannot tune-out my environment, meaning I have a species inclusive, holistic mindset which gravitates towards reverence for life, interconnectiveness, integration and wholeness.

Aspie primatologist Dawn Prince-Hughes (2005) like myself also reported a similar experience. When she integrated anarchist primitivism and ecofeminist communitarianism cross-pollinated with her Aspie identity, Prince-Hughes experienced personal and professional liberation which she *would not* have experienced otherwise. Mainly, Prince-Hughes needed community (nonhuman and human) to discover the strengths of autism and her eco-abilities (*Songs of a Gorilla Nation*).

What Is Normal? The Socio-Planetary Crisis

Disability history is linked to environmental history through the War on Nature in early modernity, orchestrated by the Enlightenment, the Age of Imperialism and the Industrial Revolution.

There are two intersections between disability and environmental history.

The first intersection is that the various disability and neurodiversity communities where all swept-up in the European War on Nature in colonial times (scientific, medical and industrial revolutions, capitalism and homogenization).

This was accomplished through the establishment of the modern mental institution to separate Western discontents from our own communities. Where we were forced against our will to reject our own Nature-based, land-based and animal-based inclinations through violent socialization, forcing us to conform to and assimilate into urbanization, industrialization, secularism, individualism, consumerism and middle class morality (the historical purpose of social work, therapy, psychiatry, mental hospitals and eugenics).

All of this did not happen just in the distant past. In fact, even in my own lifetime, even into adulthood, I am now 37-years-old, I was threatened with institutionalization even after graduating Cum Laude from the university and therapists attempted behavior modification and psychiatrists experimented with dangerous medication regimes through graduate school. Even tell this day, many professionals and parent groups still subscribe to applied behavioral analysis and I have been given emotional scars for life.

The second intersection most directly impacts the twenty-first century.

Critical Environmental Studies is in a consensus that *the status quo* is causing the socio-planetary crisis, threatening human and planetary survival, *is not* working for anyone especially oppressed minority groups around the world and we are currently calling for systematic, structural, cultural changes in human society as the only viable solution for saving humanity and Earth.

This means that *normal* and *morality is not the same thing!*

What, we the neurodiverse, then are being called to conform to is not only neurotypical insanity, we are also being pressured by the mental establishment to conform to the very system which is destroying All Life on Earth. This has led to our own addictive overconsumption, self-absorption and implication in global oppression, giving us a contaminated self, in the process.

As a result, we too need to go into "Recovery from Western Civilization" (Glendenning, 1994) through embracing the socio-planetary agenda and taking back our identities.

Subverting the Machine—The Gift of Neurodiversity

Yet, by *neurodiversity* daring to question normalcy (being superficial, indifferent, cliquish and assimilated), while also helping to keep alive the premodern Western consciousness (being introspective, sensitive, balanced and detailed-oriented) which has helped humans live sustainably with Earth for tens-of-thousands of years, coupled with some of us advocating for Animals and Earth at great pains to ourselves, we are offering a gift to Life on Earth.

In other words, we have one of the ecological visions necessary for building a sustainable future for us all.

When we cannot make all-technology go away, some of us have found ways to subvert existing harmful technologies into being in service of All Life, surviving, reproducing and flourishing, subverting these technologies away from being used toward planetary annihilation.

When we neurodiverse individuals of good will cannot make these technologies benign, we then step-it-up on questioning these technologies, for that is how technological innovations happen. Innovations happen through questioning.

Meaning it is in fact morally consistent to both question a particular technology and use that technology in your everyday life. This is what it means to live in a democracy. You speak your mind, you vote your conscience and you cope with the collective outcome.

To the best of our abilities, one thing we as neurodiverse individuals could do to decrease our carbon footprint is to divest ourselves from the overconsumption which does not help us to survive, reproduce, flourish and live with dignity. We as individuals will need to discern for ourselves as individuals, how exactly, we are to reduce our overconsumption.

We could also choose to get ourselves informed, reconnect with the Natural World, try to reconnect with the global human community, get involved with the socio-planetary movement or focus on an aspect of the socio-planetary agenda which we are passionate about.

This is because neurodiversity *is* moral! Collective Autism *is really* Collective Wildness!

References

Glendenning, C. (1990). *When technology wounds: The human consequences of progress.* New York, NY: William Marrow &Co.

Glendenning, C. (1994). *My name is Chellis Glendenning and I am in recovery from Western civilization.* Boulder, CO: Shambhala Press.

Glendenning, C. (2002). *Off the map: An expedition deep into empire and the global economy.* Gabriola Island, BC: New Society Publishers.

Glendenning, C. (2005). *Chiva: A village takes on the global heron trade.* Gabriola Island, BC: New Society Publishers.

Hughes, J. D. (1996). *Pan's travail: Environmental problems of the ancient Greeks and Romans.* Baltimore, MD: John Hopkin's University Press.

McFague, S. (1982). *Metaphoric theology: Models of God in religious language.* Philadelphia, PA: Fortress Press.

McFague, S. (2000a). *Life abundant (the search for a new framework).* Minneapolis, MN: Fortress Press.

McFague, S. (2000b). *Super, natural Christians: How we should love nature.* Minneapolis, MN: Fortress Press.

McFague, S. (2007). *A new climate for theology: God, the world and global warming.* Minneapolis, MN: Fortress Press.

Merchant, C. (1990). *The death of nature: Women, ecology and the scientific revolution.* New York, NY: HarperOne.
Prince-Hughes, D. (2005). *Songs of the gorilla nation: My journey through autism.* New York, NY: Broadway.
Zerzan, J. (2012). *Future primitive revisited.* Port Townsend, WA: Feral House
Zerzan, J. (2015). *Why hope? The stand against civilization.* Port Townsend, WA: Feral House.
Zerzan, J. (2018). *A people's history of civilization.* Port Townsend, WA: Feral House.

4. I Fled to the Wilderness and Was Surprised by Enlightenment

Daniel Salomon

I am a neurodiverse man in a neurotypical world who does not fit in.

Since a small child, I have been consistently lured into Nature for refuge and relief from a hostile, alien society, where I was free to be myself. A place where I was not controlled judged or bullied for being different.

Nature was a place where I could engage in his childhood fantasy play, where I had this inclination to personify inanimate objects, seeing inanimate objects as alive.

I learned latter that he was under the spell of an unconscious narrative called organic cosmology. A belief held by First Nation societies around the world, every Eastern religion and even every Western religion up tell the Western Enlightenment. Organic Cosmology is a belief that the Universe is alive, even inanimate objects.

These childhood experiences led me personally to self-acceptance and a massive religious conversation.

Politically, these experiences gave me, my professional vocation of grassroots political activism in defense of Animals and the Earth.

I am going to recount specific places which provided me with empowerment as a neurodiverse human. I will also talk about the role each of these places played in initiating me into a life of good works.

My First Home in the Wilderness: Tower Oaks Wilderness Area

Tower Oaks Wilderness Area was a 210-acre unprotected forest, wetland and stream valley within walking distance of my childhood home in Rockville Maryland. Tower Oaks, what I called Tower Oaks Wilderness Area, growing-up, was my childhood hide-out.

Tower Oaks was also the target of a city stormwater management project.

At age eleven, I engaged in my first environmental campaign where I collaborated with local environmental leaders. I testified before the Rockville City Council. I was also interviewed on National Public Radio. I even drew a sketch of a Blackburnian Warbler which was published in a local Audubon society newsletter.

We were successful in stopping the stormwater management proposal.

We saved a stand of old-growth trees. We saved a twelve acre wooded wetland. We saved a stretch of stream valley. We even saved a part of the Chesapeake Bay Watershed.

All of which is still here even tell this day.

I learned from my first home in the wilderness about the interconnectiveness of the Natural World. I also developed a sense of place and I was initiated into the environmental movement.

My Second Home in the Wilderness: The Places Which Inspired Mother of the Environmental Movement, Rachel Carson

The state of Maryland had a community service requirement for high school graduation when I was a youth. I completed my high school community service hours through the Rachel Carson Council. As my community service project, I explored with my family, the places which inspired mother of the environmental movement, Rachel Carson (1998a, 1998b, 2002).

We traveled from Beaufort North Carolina to Boothbay Maine. We even had the opportunity to stay a week in Rachel Carson's summer cottage outside of Boothbay in Maine where I was given the opportunity to explore Rachel Carson's own tide pools and Rachel Carson's own fairyland of lichens. I even was given the opportunity to set-up my own microscope on Rachel Carson's own desk.

Out of my high school community service project, I self-published my first book through the Rachel Carson Council (Salomon, 1997), where I sold over 200 copies, raising money for the Rachel Carson Council, in the process. My book was even used as part of a curriculum in a Northern Virginia public elementary school.

I learned from my second home in the wilderness about my sense of wonder toward the Natural World. I also learned from my second wilderness home about the types of discriminations and persecutions which women and marginalized groups experience when they advocate for the planet and humanity.

My Third Home in the Wilderness: The Salisbury Zoo

I gained not only the ability to teach the public about animals and the environment, but I even gained the ability to engage in interspecies communications when I volunteered one summer in the Salisbury Zoo in Salisbury Maryland, when I was an undergraduate at Salisbury University.

I gained interspecies communications abilities when I reached-out and prayed with a Canada goose with a broken wing named Wounded Healer who I developed an interspecies friendship with and followed through the years.

I developed both my interspecies communication abilities and my ability to teach and work with the general public when I read, studied and attempted to practice the various Judeo-Christian spiritualities of interspecies communications including the Franciscan tradition.

All of these Judeo-Christian interspecies communication traditions were based on the premise that the Natural World as well as humanity is basically good and that it is possible to not only restore human relations, it is even possible to restore human-nonhuman relationships.

I learned from my third home in the wilderness about the goodness of humanity and the existence of interspecies communications.

My Fourth Home in the Wilderness: Deer Ridge

I came back home to Maryland after graduating from graduate school in the Boston area. Several years later, I moved out to an apartment in the outer suburbs of Washington D.C., adjacent to a major state park to recover from burn-out after going through a whole slew of discrimination situations because of my disability.

I lived adjacent to the state park for two years. During these two years, I ended-up cleaning-up garbage in a nearby forest and stream valley. A handmade sign posted by an anonymous neighbor named this neglected place, Deer Ridge.

Within two years, I was able to transform this abandoned town dump into a beautiful community resource and vibrant wildlife sanctuary.

I learned from my fourth home in the wilderness a new appreciation for manual labor, the invigoration of physical exercise, the pride of good craftsmanship, the necessity of engaging in practical environmental work, the joy of "protecting life and beauty" (Pope Francis), the happiness of getting out of myself and my problems, the reward of seeing the fruits of my own labor and the connection between meaningful work and human dignity. Most importantly, I learned from my forth home in the wilderness that I was not powerless over my own environment. I could transform my environment through creative actions and hard work. Cleaning-up Deer Ridge felt like I was restoring a beautiful work of art. I really felt empowered in my fourth home in the wilderness. I even felt less lonely when I was working in Deer Ridge.

My Fifth Home in the Wilderness: Portland, Oregon

My parents gave me the opportunity to visit Portland, Oregon on a family vacation about five years ago. When we visited Portland, I felt like Portland was my spiritual home. I felt like I just found the green community which I had been searching for, for over a decade.

I felt like Portland was my spiritual home not only because Portland was one of the epicenters for the environmental movement. I have never been to a city which was so welcoming to strangers. Portlanders were so laid-back and down-to-earth.

I wanted to move to Portland.

Two years later, I was able to relocate to Portland with my parents.

I now live in Portland. I am now a Portlander.

Becoming a Portlander really turned my life around. Becoming a Portlander was a real life-changing experience for me.

I learned from my fifth home in the wilderness what it is like to be part of an authentic community, to work together towards a common goal, the necessity of livability, scalability even belonging for my physical and mental well-being and the possibility of being less competitive, more laid-back and more myself in community. I also learned in my fifth home in the wilderness that I could do anything. I learned this for the first time in my life.

In my fifth home in the wilderness, I was able to fit into a human community for the first time in my life.

My Sixth Home in the Wilderness: Block Seven

Shortly after moving to Portland, my beautiful new home was under threat by invading developers. A club for rich people in my new neighborhood wanted to sell off an entire block of their land to developers in a sweetheart deal.

If this proposal went through, it would have destroyed the last remaining open green space in the neighborhood, a place which the City of Portland called Block Seven.

Despite powerful opposition on all sides, I banded together with my fellow neighbors and after working very hard, together, taking all kinds of different calculated risks and creative actions on behalf of Block Seven and the surrounding neighborhood, we were able to get the developers and the club to withdraw their proposal. Block Seven remains undeveloped, even tell this day. By saving Block Seven from development, we were able to not only protect a block of open green space, coupled with a stand of mature trees and shrubs, we were also able to protect the environmental sustainability, human livability and historical character of our neighborhood, in the process.

I learned from my sixth home in the wilderness about the importance of not giving-up or giving-in too quickly. Of not being intimidated by the fear of failure or by powerful opposition. That taking calculating risks despite uncertainty is in-fact the most realistic option for moving forward. That winning is not everything. That success is not everything. Faithfulness is more important. In the end, we can still win and be successful.

Block Seven also put a face on the moral bankruptcy of consumerism and individualism in North America where I witnessed firsthand the sense of entitlement of the superrich and how the land and the common good were being treated as a legal non-entity. I witnessed firsthand all the political, economic and legal barriers individual citizens of good-will are faced with when trying to effectuate change.

I also witnessed firsthand that when individual citizens of good-will band together to cooperate and work together towards a common goal, despite our seemingly irreconcile differences, we are then able to scour these political and economic barriers even legal barriers.

I learn from saving Block Seven that working together as a human community is essential for effectuating change on behalf of the planet and humanity.

I also learned from saving Block Seven that working together as a team is something I could also participate in and contribute to. This is something I could do. This is something I did do. I pulled-it off in real life!

My Seventh Home in the Wilderness: Hoyt Arboretum

Since I moved to Portland, I built-up enough strength and confidence to start volunteering in the community.

After exploring the great ecological institutions of Portland, I found the Hoyt Arboretum in Washington Park to be a good fit for volunteering. Not only did I have long-standing abilities in natural history, working with plants versus animals, meant I could work on a clean conscience. I would not need to participate in practices which would be part of work, which involved harming or killing animals in anyway. Harming and killing animals in a volunteer or employment situation is against my conscience. Many of the volunteering and paid jobs in the animal field involved doing just that. Harming and killing animals.

I walked into the visit center, filled-out a volunteer application and met with the volunteer coordinator. I was accepted as a volunteer tour guide and I switched my focus from animals to plants.

With time, I was trained to also become a herbarium archive assistant and citizen scientist by the arboretum's plant taxonomist. I also have been able to give lectures even lead entire workshops.

I have even been able to lead all-access special needs tours for peoples with disabilities.

I have been volunteering at the Hoyt Arboretum for over three years and counting.

In my seventh home in the wilderness I have been able to use knowledge I learned in school. Master practical skills in my field, work in my field, dialogue with and be mentored by people in my field. Teach, lead and mentor myself. Have some of my non-profit innovations be accepted and implemented by an organization and be able to research and implement constructive environmental solutions. I even have been able to overcome my fears of volunteering and paid employment in my seventh home in the wilderness.

My Eighth Home in the Wilderness: Pittock Mansion

One of the places I really liked in Portland was the Pittock Mansion. The Pittock Mansion with its bird's eye panoramic view of the entire city of Portland surrounded by the Cascade Mountains with snowcapped Mount Hood towering over and framed by a moist lush temperate rainforest which encloses a vast vibrant fecund garden, embodied my childhood fantasy of what an idyllic Pacific Northwest garden estate would look like. An enchanted garden!

I started volunteering at the Pittock Mansion earlier this year, combining my love of history and my newfound respect for historical preservation with my personal response to the human ecology dimensions of Pope Francis's Encyclical (Pope Francis, 2015).

As a result, I gravitated to hosting the gate lodge at the Pittock Mansion, where Pittock's steward or groundskeeper live with his wife and daughter.

I really like hosting the gate lodge for two reasons. First, the gate lodge preserved how an ordinary family lived in the olden days. Second, Pittock's steward embodied the archetype, the common human experience, of Caring for Creation which has been adopted by the Christian religion as an alternative interpretation to dominion meaning domination in the Old Testament.

I also sought solace in my eighth home in the wilderness when I was working to save Block Seven from overdevelopment. The Pittock family provided an alternative way to be superrich. The Pittock's who came from a Unitarian background treated all their employees fairly and justly, engaged in community service and philanthropy, used local building when possible when building their estate and did not live an excessively extravagant lifestyle. Also, the entire Pittock estate and grounds were saved from demolition by a grassroots effort of local citizens of good will. These two alternative possibilities gave me the inspiration to carry on in my struggle to save Block 7 from overdevelopment.

Conclusion

I originally fled to the Natural World to escape loneness and alienation. I was surprised by being taught how I could re-integrate myself back into my community and fulfill my dream of becoming a Roman Catholic Christian.

References

Carson, R. (1998a). *The sense of wonder*. New York, NY: Harper Reprint.
Carson, R. (1998b). *The edge of the sea*. Wilmington, MA: Mariner Books.
Carson, R. (2002). *Silent spring*. Boston, MA: Houghton Muffin Company.
Francis, P. (2015). *Laudato si: On care for our common home*. Huntington, IN: Our Sunday Visitor.
Salomon, D. (1997). *Rachel Carson in Carteret County, North Carolina: A journey to the edge of the sea*. Bethesda, MD: Rachel Carson Council, Inc.

5. Post-Structural Analyses of Conformity and Oppression: A Discussion of Critical Animal Studies and Neurodiversity

Hannah Monroe

This chapter explores the discursive construction of normative behavior and non-conformity. I will discuss theories about normativity from a post-structural perspective, particularly focusing on critical disability theory. I will then describe the discursive processes of medicalization, focusing on neurodiversity and autism. After outlining theory on difference and medicalization from critical disability studies, I will focus specifically on neurodiversity. My analysis of neurodiversity as a site of non-conformity will primarily focus on autism, as this is the focus of my thesis research. Then I will apply these ideas to critical animal studies, exploring the ways nonhuman animals are non-conforming in relation to discursive norms. This includes the discursive construction of humanness, and how notions of what it means to be human function not only to oppress animals, but also humans who are constituted as deviating from the normative notion of the human. To close this chapter, I will discuss the possibilities for non-human animals to be included in ideas of neurodiversity, in the ways they resist human norms.

My graduate research focuses on neurodiversity, and autism specifically, though thinking about the social construction of normalcy is helpful for questioning other dominant discourses around disability as well. I want to explore what questioning normalcy is like in LGBTQIA and disability rights activism. Furthermore, this view of questioning normalcy can be helpful in thinking about nonhuman animals and their agency. Thus, this chapter will discuss a post-structural view of non-conformity from both neurodiverse and critical animal studies perspectives. Normalcy and non-conformity have been concepts that interested me for most of my life. Throughout my undergraduate academic work, I focused on gender expression and performance. However, in studying gender norms, I was always aware that there was something else beyond gender that I was drawn to exploring. Beyond my interest in gender was an interest in understanding the oppression and experience of non-conformity. This realization, in combination with an internship I did in disability rights, brought me to critical disability studies and specifically neurodiversity.

This chapter draws connections between neurodiversity and eco-ability, which is a field of study at the intersection of critical animal, environmental, and disability studies that was created by Anthony J. Nocella II (Socha, Bentley, & Schatz, 2014, pp. 1–2). This chapter follows previous literature on eco-ability, which includes the anthology *Earth, Animal and Disability Liberation: The Rise of the Eco-ability Movement* and three special journal issues (Eccles, Nocella, & Socha, 2015; Juergensmeyer, 2016; Nocella, Bentley, & Duncan, 2012; Socha, Bentley, & Schatz, 2014).

Post-structural Theory and Discourse

In *Disability Studies: An Interdisciplinary Introduction*, Goodley defines discourses as "regulated systems of statements, ideas and practices, providing ways of representing particular forms of knowledge, which we use to shape the subjective sense of who we and others are" (Goodley, 2011, p. 103). Discourses produce binaries, constructing one category as the opposite of the other, with each supporting the discursive positioning of the other (Goodley, 2011, p. 104). Goodley writes that the normative identity is privileged, with disabled identities otherized in comparison to the norm. Neurotypicality is normalized through the pathologizing of neurodiversity (Goodley, 2011, pp. 104–105).

People embody discourses, constructing their knowledge of themselves and their behaviors around the ways they are made to feel knowable. In this way, the self is constructed through discourse. People only feel knowable through certain discourses because they are reproduced and pervade our entire lives through medicine, school, work, and many other institutions (Goodley, 2011, p. 106). This can be observed particularly clearly in discourses surrounding mental and neurological disability through psychiatry and special education perpetuating the view of neurodiverse people as "other." Neurodiverse people are taught this perspective as their subjectivities are constituted through discourse by these institutions. This teaching of the dominant discourse is related to notions of power in post-structural theory. In the introduction to *Foucault and the Government of Disability*, Shelley Tremain explains Foucault's notions of power as "not something that is exchanged, given, or taken back, but rather is *exercised* and exists only in action" (Tremain, 2005, p. 4). Power exists in society through discourse; through internalizing and performing normativity or through developing counter discourses to resist norms.

Individuals who are constructed as non-normative in multiple ways, such as neurodiverse people of color, often experience more oppression by dominant discourses that privilege neurotypicality and whiteness (Goodley, 2011, p. 105). People's experiences of disability, as well as any kind of non-conformity to dominant discursive norms, are closely connected to sexuality, gender, race, and class. Anne McGuire writes that ableism affects individuals differently based on intersections of identity and thus disability is socially experienced in different ways (McGuire, 2016, p. 17).

Normalcy

In McGuire's recent book *War on Autism: On the Cultural Logic of Normative Violence*, she provides an excellent post-structural analysis of the discursive constructions of normalcy regarding autism (McGuire, 2016). McGuire suggests that mainstream advocacy discourse constructs autism as a threat to normative society (McGuire, 2016, pp. 21, 112). She asserts that autism advocacy's role within this narrative is to maintain normalcy, preserving it from the ever present threat of non-conformity (McGuire, 2016, p. 141). Autistic non-conformity is constructed as not just an individual issue, but as a threat to capitalism itself (McGuire, 2016, pp. 112–113). Nocella also asserts that those who are constructed as "different," are regarded as "a threat that must be controlled, disciplined, and punished" (2012, p. 5). Within the dominant discourse, those outside the norm are thus regarded as threatening to normativity and subjected to forms of control and repression (Nocella, 2012, p. 5).

Interestingly, McGuire tells us that what autism advocacy organizations label as signs of pathology are often behaviors that are "both 'too much' and 'not enough'" (McGuire, 2016, p. 95). Thus, people are perceived as deviant when they are performing a normative behavior excessively or too little. This can be observed in how autistic people are often viewed as either too rational or too emotional. They are pathologized for not meeting the specific balance of rationality and emotionality constructed as normal. In "Autism as Culture," Joseph N. Straus makes this observation as well. He asserts that many psychiatric disorders diagnose expressions and behaviors that, at certain levels, would be considered normative, but are constructed as deviant when they exceed past this line of normalcy. For example, autistic people are pathologized for being too independent, despite society idealizing a certain level of independence for its citizens (Straus, 2013, p. 461). In "Popular Discourses on the Neurotypical Woman: Conformity, Authority, and Post-War Femininities," Nancy Bombaci also argues that the dominant discursive constitution of Asperger's pathologizes people who are independent and demonstrate an aptitude for intellectualism. She argues that this discourse especially pathologizes women for having these characteristics (Bombaci, 2012, pp. 140–141).

The pathologizing of non-conforming characteristics of autistic people perpetuates stigma against gender non-conformity. Davidson and Tamas (2016) assert that in diagnostic materials, autistic people are often described as deviating from social norms in gendered ways, providing the example of Simon Baron-Cohen's theory of the "extreme male brain." This theory claims that autistic people tend to be more masculine, and clearly genders autistic non-conformity (Davidson & Tamas, 2016, p. 60). There may be a connection between autism and gender non-conformity because, as Davidson and Tamas describe, in "Autism and the Ghost of Gender," autistic people "apparently do not fall under gender's spell quite so readily" (2016, p. 62). This is largely because autism is defined by difficulty in understanding social norms, so gender norms are less likely to be understood and followed as well (Davidson & Tamas, 2016, p. 62). However, an assumption that gender non-conformity is a "symptom" of autism pathologizes the gender expression of any autistic person who does not follow gender norms.

Discursive constructions of normalcy are often maintained through the medicalization of non-conformity. We can observe the dominance of the medical discourse in the twentieth century through the vast amount of social phenomena that have been medicalized as opposed to de-medicalized (Oliver, 1990, p. 50). The belief that people need medical treatment to "cure" their differences has prevailed in Western culture. Goodley asserts this constructed ideal is based on norms of productivity (Goodley, 2011, p. 114). As people's abilities have become perceived as unproductive within capitalist society, they have been pathologized to be objects of social control. Citing Foucault, Oliver explains that those characterized as "mad have been excluded from normal social life and isolated in a specialist domain" (Oliver, 1990, p. 47). McGuire asserts as well that disability is only intelligible in the dominant discourse as a dangerous deficiency that needs to be protected against (McGuire, 2016, p. 15).

Neurodiversity

McGee (2012) provides a definition of neurodiversity that highlights its counter discursive potential, writing:

> The most vocal advocates for neurodiversity have been persons whom the medical, psychiatric, and educational domains would categorize as autistic or "on the autism spectrum." But the movement also includes those with neurological differences as varied as ADHD, Alzheimer's disease, bipolar disorder, dyslexia, dyspraxia, depression, epilepsy, Tourette's syndrome, and any number of other psychiatric and neurological classifications. (p. 12)

This definition fits particularly well in a poststructuralist theoretical framework, as McGee emphasizes that individuals are categorized or classified as diagnoses outlined in *The Diagnostic and Statistical Manual of Mental Disorders (DSM)*. This description of medical, psychiatric, and educational institutions categorizing individuals according to discursively constituted labels is central to a post-structural analysis. Eco-ability takes this perspective as well, critiquing discursive categories, especially those around notions of "normalcy" (Socha, Bentley, & Schatz, 2014, p. 2).

It is also important to address the social model of disability, which McGuire asserts is often employed by disability scholars and activists, but has had some critiques. The social model distinguishes between impairment, one's physical differences, and disability, the ways society privileges able-bodied people over disabled people. However, McGuire describes how some people have critiqued the distinction between these two aspects of disabled experience as well as the presentation as objective fact that some bodies are physically different. She also cites Shelley Tremain's assertion that we should not accept the notion of impairment as impartial, as this label carries political and discursive power (McGuire, 2016, p. 16).

While the intention of the social model's narrative is to counter the medical model of disability, the social model's use of categories and distinctions to describe disabled experiences continues to naturalize binary discourses about disability. It is crucial to question naturalized norms and distinctions such as these, just as we question the idea of the human in critical animal studies. Eco-ability works to critique binaries and the discursive categorizing of human and non-human animals into dualistic groups. Socha, Bentley, and Schatz assert that we must maintain an awareness of and work to deconstruct all oppressive, hierarchal dualisms (Socha, Bentley, & Schatz, 2014, p. 3). As dualisms so often privilege one side as "normal," continuing to think in terms of disabled/non-disabled or neurodiverse/neurotypical risks perpetuating harmful discourses. Furthermore, the eco-ability movement seeks to question categories that divide us (Socha, Bentley, & Schatz, 2014, p. 2). Thinking of ourselves as existing in distinct categories is neither realistic nor helpful for working towards social justice. Describing being neurodiverse as an identity, even while creating alternative discourse to the dominant discursive categories of mental disability, still represents neurodiverse individuals as different from people considered non-disabled.

McGuire takes a specifically post-structural perspective in how she discusses the concept of autism, asserting that it is not a specifically definable category, but is instead always shifting in its culturally constructed meanings (McGuire, 2016, p. 21). This view of disability and neurodiversity is post-structural, as it highlights the complexity and fluidity of concepts such as disability, difference, normality, and abnormality. The concept of neurodiversity is a helpful way to think about mental difference, as long as it does not rely on a binary of neurodiverse/neurotypical.

Discourses of Neurodiversity

Neurodiversity is part of a counter discursive construction of autism, as well as many other mental and neurological differences or disabilities. For the remainder of this discussion of discourse and neurodiversity, I will focus on autism because it seems to be at the center of current discursive conflict in media and culture, and serves as a useful case study. Alicia Broderick and Ari Ne'eman write that in the early 2000s autism in particular took hold of "the public imagination internationally" becoming a "popular cultural obsession" (Broderick & Ne'eman, 2008, p. 462). It is significant to note that the dominant discourse constituting autism as a disease is primarily rooted in the non-autistic community, whereas the counter discourse promoting neurodiversity and constituting autism as difference is rooted in the autistic and neurodiverse community (Broderick & Ne'eman, 2008, p. 468). Broderick and Ne'eman explain that discourse is integral to the production of power/knowledge (Broderick & Ne'eman, 2008, p. 460). They argue this discursive struggle is so critical because the human rights of autistic people are at stake (Broderick & Ne'eman, 2008, p. 474).

Dominant Discourse of Autism

The dominant discursive construction of autism is the focus of McGuire's book, *War on Autism*. Drawing on Ian Hacking, McGuire writes that as "contemporary stories of autism" help construct discourse, they "are, in other words, functioning to constitute what autism is and can be" (McGuire, 2016,

p. 11). The most powerful proponent of the dominant discourse is Autism Speaks, an organization widely criticized by the neurodiverse advocacy and autistic communities (Broderick & Ne'eman, 2008, pp. 468, 472). McGuire argues that these stories are all interconnected in "contributing to the formation of a historically specific autism discourse" (McGuire, 2016, p. 12). These narratives come together to construct an overarching discourse of autism.

Tremain describes how discursive classifications organize people based on how they exist in relation to constituted norms, and so construct social identity and social organization. This awareness of one's identity in relation to norms is a subject's "conscience or self-knowledge" (Tremain, 2005, p. 6). Practices to become more normal are then offered within culture to individuals, as they are encouraged to change themselves to more closely resemble normalcy. People are expected to want to change and to accept these forms of normalization (Tremain, 2005, p. 8). He describes how people perform what the dominant discourse defines as normativity, policing their thoughts and behaviors (McGuire, 2016, p. 73). Those who are non-conforming become medicalized within scientific and psychological discourses and have their differences devalued as merely part of a pathological condition. The pathologizing of autistic non-conformity discursively constrains autistic individuals from claiming and embracing autism as part of their identities (McGuire, 2016, p. 7). People regulate their performance according to social norms in order to be intelligible, or knowable, within dominant cultural discourse (McGuire, 2016, p. 73). Despite the cultural dominance of thinking about autism this way, many people have criticized this medicalizing normative discourse.

Counter Discourse and the Neurodiversity Movement

Drawing on Hacking, McGuire emphasizes sharing counter discourses, such as through stories from autistic individuals, promotes alternative narratives of autism in culture (McGuire, 2016, p. 11). This can broaden intelligibility for autistic people, rendering their ways of living and thinking more visible. However, she reminds us that, while narratives alternative to the dominant stories about autism do exist, dominant narratives are held as objectively true while counter narratives are often disregarded (McGuire, 2016, p. 13). The dominant discourse gains its strength in culture from its attachment to science and medicine, which are powerful institutions in our society (Broderick & Ne'eman, 2008, p. 469). Those representing the dominant discourse are legitimized as authority figures, enabling them to devalue the perspectives of autistic individuals and anyone else who questions the dominant narratives of disease and normalcy (McGuire, 2016, p. 13).

However, McGuire argues that "autistic perspectives in disability theory are reconfiguring how autistic difference is perceived and, indeed, how it can be imagined" (McGuire, 2016, p. 18). This ability to contribute counter discursive perspectives to the cultural conception of disability is a powerful site for resistance. The neurodiversity movement promotes a counter discourse of autism along with other mental and neurological differences, questioning the supposed legitimacy of medical discourse and the pathologizing of non-conformity. In her article "Quirky Citizens: Autism, Gender, and Reimagining Disability," Bumiller argues this is ultimately a social movement about issues of normalcy and broadening intelligibility. As such, it provides implications for gender studies and feminist theory. Her assertion that autism "is in fact medically defined by an inability to understand social conventions" (Bumiller, 2008, p. 976) highlights a connection between social norms, unintelligibility, and disablement.

Just as counter discourses from the neurodiversity movement, and critical disability studies, seek to question the constructions of disability and normative existence, critical animal studies questions the notions of humanness and animality. Eco-ability bridges these two perspectives, as discussed by Nocella in his chapter "Defining Eco-Ability" in *Earth, Animal, and Disability Liberation*. Eco-ability exists at the intersection of the environmental, animal liberation, and disability rights movements (Nocella, 2012, p. 9). Eco-ability shares the neurodiversity movement's goal of deconstructing the idea of normalcy. Nocella explains that "these concepts are social constructions that fail to respect the uniqueness of individual abilities and differences" (2012, p. 5). In the eco-ability movement's work to embrace diversity, it clearly allies with the neurodiversity movement as previously outlined. Critical animal studies and eco-ability look at the ways dominant discursive constructions of humanness lead to oppression of marginalized people as well as non-human animals. Furthermore, applying the aforementioned post-structural analyses of discursive constructions of normalcy, disability, and autism to critical animal studies can yield some interesting results.

Neurodiversity and Critical Animal Studies

One of the most important discursive connections between disability and animal rights is how the idea of humanness is constructed within ableist discourse. The concept of humanness is connected to dominant discourse of normative development, as is discussed by McGuire in *War on Autism*. She asserts that to be understood as human by the dominant discourse within the binary of human/non-human is to behave in a normative way. Thus, autistic people are then viewed as "partially developed, and thus as not fully human" (McGuire, 2016, p. 91). Humanness is perceived as a state that one must achieve, and thus can be taught if one has the potential to be completely human (McGuire, 2016, p. 91). When discussing the "signs of autism," McGuire describes these as constructions of what it means to be human (McGuire, 2016, p. 98). As signs of supposedly abnormal human behavior, these guides of what people are expected to watch out for designate who is fully performing humanness. People, are then, only accepted as fully human when they are no longer expressing any elements of so-called non-normative autism (McGuire, 2016, p. 101). Bergenmar, Rosqvist, and Lönngren also assert that what is considered disabling about autism by the dominant discourse is connected not only to norms around ability, but also to the very idea of humanness (Bergenmar, Rosqvist, & Lönngren, 2015, p. 203). From a broader disability studies perspective, Nocella asserts that many marginalized groups have been compared to animals or disabled people as a form of oppression. This issue of people being oppressed through comparisons to non-human animals demonstrates connections between discrimination against marginalized human groups and the devaluation and oppression of non-human animals, as well as that of disabled people (Nocella, 2012, p. 4).

Another connection between critical animal studies and neurodiversity is the way that people's friendships with nonhuman animals are perceived as somehow not "real" and a sign of disability. Although it is a stereotype that autistic people get along well with animals, some people relate to it and we need to think about why this as regarded as inferior to human friendships. Getting along better with nonhuman animals than with humans is constructed as not normatively social. We can observe this in how people who live with animals, but don't have family or housemates, are labeled as lonely or as somehow mentally ill. The tendency to value human companionship over living only with nonhuman animals is a sign of speciesism as well as ableism. Drawing on Dunayer, Nocella defines speciesism as "discrimination against nonhuman animal species by arguing that humans are more important and superior to nonhuman animals" (Nocella, 2012, p. 8). The devaluation of people's friendships with nonhuman animals, in comparison to those with humans, is rooted in the belief that we cannot have equally meaningful social interactions with nonhuman animals, because they are regarded as less socially important. We need to think critically about both the speciesism and ableism embedded in narratives around human and nonhuman animal friendships.

Bergenmar, Rosqvist, and Lönngren discuss these friendships and connections between autistic people and nonhuman animals in "Autism and the Question of the Human." They look at several autobiographies of autistic individuals and analyze the way these authors talk about animals. For example, Dawn Prince-Hughes, a primatologist, found that gorillas understood her in ways she never felt understood by other humans (Bergenmar et al., 2015, p. 207). Wolfe also addresses neurodiversity and identity as it relates to animals, when he describes a few autistic people who say they can relate to animals because of their different abilities, such as Temple Grandin and Monty Roberts. I thought it was particularly interesting to read about how Roberts learned more about herself and her unique perspectives by being around gorillas, as this suggests animals may be allies in a way for people with disabilities (Wolfe, 2008, p. 111). These are experiences of solidarity between neurodiverse people and non-human animals that should be valued. People who are non-conforming may be able to find support from non-human animals because they might relate to animals' non-conformity to human neurotypical culture, and vice versa.

Bergenmar, Rosqvist, and Lönngren take a post-humanist approach and look at discourses around autism and the notions of humans and "animals" (Bergenmar et al., 2015, p. 203). They assert that the autistic people they write about, such as Dawn Prince-Hughes, question the dualistic categories of humans and non-human animals by critiquing what it means to follow norms of interaction with others. As some of these individuals comment that they feel close to animals, they also destabilize this dualistic view. These authors argue that in this way both constructions of normalcy as well as of humanness and animalness are called into question (Bergenmar et al., 2015, p. 215). The view of some of these individuals that they may feel more of a connection to animals than other people calls into question what supposedly makes humans different from nonhuman animals (Bergenmar et al., 2015, p. 211).

The last point I would like to make about connections we can draw between critical disability and animal studies is to look at ways non-human animals could be viewed as neurodiverse, in a culture that pathologizes any deviance from human norms. For example, I have been thinking lately about neurodiversity in nonhuman animals and the ways they don't conform to human social norms. When they do things that humans don't understand, they are often described as "cute," while the same behavior would be stigmatized in autistic people. A little while ago I was playing with a cat, who was so happy and excited that she stopped playing and ran around the room. This is a thing that many cats and dogs do, but in thinking about this chapter, it occurred to me that this is also something many autistic people do when happiness from interests or positive thoughts creates a burst of energy. We have all most likely observed cats and other animals stim, forms of movement neurodiverse people use to manage both positive and negative emotional experiences. Examples of stimming include cats kneading with their paws and purring to calm themselves and express contentment.

It is important to note that in relation to the standards our society places on people and non-human animals, they could in many ways be perceived as neurodiverse. People often punish their pets for engaging in behavior that could be perceived as non-conforming, when it becomes somehow inconvenient for the humans they live with. As mentioned before, many people perceive seemingly weird things non-human animals do as "cute," infantilizing them. However, their behavior can sometimes cross a line at which it stops being cute and becomes a "problem." Examples include cats scratching on furniture and animals who are so anxious, or perhaps introverted, that they avoid being around the humans they live with. There is an expectation that they should be social and entertain people. It is important to think about what these expectations and beliefs about differences in animals say about both speciesism and ableism in our society.

Conclusion

I would like to end this chapter with a discussion of and call for collective resistance against these discourses of normalcy that could include human and non-human animals. Post-structural theory asserts that voicing and spreading counter discourses is a form of agency and resistance. We need to keep encouraging non-conformity and respect animals when they don't conform. Goodley asserts the goal of post-structuralism is to deconstruct binary discourses and work for discursive resistance through renaming and resignification, as discourse shapes how we think about ourselves and others (Goodley, 2011, p. 106). By continuing to voice our beliefs in the face of the dominant discourse, I think we can erode the power of oppressive ways of thinking. This is not easy and is not something everyone is able to do, but I really believe that being true to how we want to be in the world can make a difference little by little. We also need to pay attention to the ways that animals resist and respect that they can be part of resistance as well. When we notice animals being non-conforming, we need to support their individuality and agency. Humans and non-human animals can help each other resist these discourses and survive in a society that tells us it is not ok to be who we are.

References

Bergenmar, J., Rosqvist, H. B., & Lönngren, A. S. (2015). Autism and the question of the human. *Literature and Medicine, 33*(1), 202–221.

Bombaci, N. (2012). Popular discourses on the neurotypical woman: Conformity, authority, and post-war femininities. *Women: A Cultural Review, 23*(2), 139–162.

Broderick, A., & Ne'eman, A. (2008). Autism as metaphor: Narrative and counter-narrative. *International Journal of Inclusive Education, 12*(5–6), 459–476.

Bumiller, K. (2008). Quirky citizens: Autism, gender, and reimagining disability. *Signs, 33*(4), 967–991.

Davidson, J., & Tamas, S. (2016). Autism and the ghost of gender. *Emotion, Space and Society, 19*, 59–65.

Eccles, S., Nocella, A. J., & Socha, K. (Eds.). (2015). Transcripts of 2nd annual engaging with eco-ability conference [special issue]. *Green Theory and Praxis Journal, 8*(1), 1–67.

Goodley, D. (2011). *Disability studies: An interdisciplinary introduction.* Los Angeles, CA: Sage.

Juergensmeyer, E. (Ed.). (2016). Transcripts of the 3rd annual engaging with eco-ability conference [special issue]. *Green Theory and Praxis Journal, 9*(1).

McGee, M. (2012). Neurodiversity. *Contexts, 11*(3), 12–13.

McGuire, A. (2016). *War on autism: On the cultural logic of normative violence.* Ann Arbor, MI: University of Michigan Press.

Nocella II, A. J. (2012). Defining eco-ability: Social justice and the intersectionality of disability, nonhuman animals, and ecology. In A. J. Nocella, J. Bentley, & J. M. Duncan (Eds.), *Earth, animal and disability liberation: The rise of the eco-ability movement* (pp. 3–21). New York, NY: Peter Lang Publishing.

Nocella II, A. J., Bentley, J., & Duncan, J. M. (Eds.). (2012). *Earth, animal and disability liberation: The rise of the eco-ability movement.* New York, NY: Peter Lang Publishing.

Oliver, M. (1990). *The politics of disablement.* London: Macmillan Education.

Socha, K. A., Bentley, J. K. D., & Schatz, J. L. (2014). An introduction to eco-ability: The struggle for justice, with focus on humans with disabilities and nonhuman animals. *Journal for Critical Animal Studies, 12*(2), 1–8.

Straus, J. N. (2013). Autism as culture. In L. J. Davis (Ed.), *The disability studies reader* (pp. 460–484). New York, NY: Routledge.

Tremain, S. (2005). Foucault, governmentality, and critical disability theory: An introduction. In S. Tremain (Ed.), *Foucault and the government of disability* (pp. 1–24). Ann Arbor, MI: University of Michigan Press.

Wolfe, C. (2008). Learning from Temple Grandin, or, animal studies, disability studies, and who comes after the subject. *New Formations, 64*, 110–123.

6. Giving a Face to the Nameless Numbers

MARY FANTASKE

As we jogged up to where the truck was parked, the stench of blood, feces, sickness, and death slammed into our respiratory systems, forcing us to cup our hands over our mouths and noses in an effort to prevent gagging. We slowed our pace as we reached the filthy, metal truck, so as to not startle the already-terrified persyns trapped inside. I stood about a foot from the truck, gentling telling them how beautiful they were and how they were loved by those standing there with them. As I observed their responses, I knew it would now be okay to go right up to the truck and put my hands through the holes in the cold, unforgiving metal. They hung there for another few minutes while I continued conversing with those who were being treated like objects, and whose stories had been treated as if they were not only irrelevant, but non-existent. And then one of them, with handsome black hair and dark eyes so gorgeous in their depth that you could find yourself becoming lost in them, moved a little closer and pressed his forehead to my hand. I do not dramatize when I say that everything went silent, that for those few incredibly intimate and beautiful moments during which I suddenly knew him, and him me, the rest of the dark, violent place of death we found ourselves in, with its deafening mechanical sounds and blinding smell of blood, fell away. We connected in every sense of the word. And then the sounds and smells came back, smacking me in the face, as he was dragged away in the truck that would lead him to his brutal death. I held on, touching him, communicating with him, for as long as I could, once again jogging, but this time beside the truck, and this time with tears rolling down my face and off my cheeks. And that was it. That was our entire interaction. Our entire story together. And yet, it changed my life. For although I had spent years in the company of his kind living on sanctuaries, and although I had also spent years involved in ecofeminist and eco-ability discussions concerning the objectification of disabled persyns like me and animal persyns like him. However, until that moment, I had never been face to face with someone who was minutes away from being violently transformed into a literal object, and whose story was moments away from being completely erased.

In this chapter, I will argue that the systems which work to oppress ability diverse humyns as well as nonhumyn persyns, known as ableism and speciesism, are not only similar in their consequences for oppressed individuals, but hold the same problematic beliefs and assumptions as their foundations. For clarification, the letter "y" is used instead of "e", "a" or "o" in words to remove the suffixes, "men", "man" and "son", and thus not contribute to the linguistic implication that all beings must be defined by a comparison to the white, abled, cis, heterosexual, rational, humyn man. With this in mind, I argue that the number of similarities between ableism and speciesism suggests they should be combatted together rather than separately. Finally, the concepts of the ecofeminist "ethics of care" and the act of "bearing witness" will be explored as forms of subversive eco-ability activism that could play a substantive role in dismantling oppressive systems such as ableism and speciesism.

Ableism, loosely defined as the belief that a humyn persyn with certain "abilities" holds more worth than someone who is perceived as not having those "abilities," and speciesism, loosely defined as the belief that humyns are inherently more valuable than any other species, are systems which are both sociological and psychological in nature. This may seem to be a simple statement, but in order to closely examine and evaluate certain forms of subversive eco-ability action, it is of the utmost importance that we understand the socially constructed nature of these oppressive systems. In *Why We Love Dogs, Eat Pigs, and Wear Cows* author Melanie Joy (2010) describes the social and psychological features of what she calls "carnism," an ideology that allows us to feel indifferent about eating some sentient beings while feeling disgusted by the thought of eating others. The way in which Joy examines carnism is just as insightful when applied to analyzing ableism and speciesism. For Joy, the notion of the psychological schema informs how carnism works on both behavioral and systemic levels. She explains, "a schema is a psychological framework that shapes—and is shaped by—our beliefs, ideas, perceptions, and experiences, and it automatically organizes and interprets incoming information" (Joy, 2010, p. 14). She proceeds to state that generalizations largely arise from schemas; "generalizations are the result of schemas doing what they're supposed to: sorting through and interpreting the vast number of stimuli we're constantly exposed to and then putting it into general categories. Schemas act as mental classification systems" (Joy, 2010, p. 14). Although we are not born with the schemas we hold as adults, it is fair to say that the tendency to create schemas or the need to classify, is something innate to the human species. Thus we naturally, and without effort, internalize belief systems/ideologies leading to the formulation of schemas. However, the drive to categorize phenomena is not what is problematic. Indeed, the capability to create schemas allows for the potential of faster thought-processes, something which can be of particular benefit when, for example, one is trying to discern whether something should be categorized as a threat. Schemas, as psychological constructions, are not inherently problematic and do not necessarily produce discriminative thoughts or actions, but it unfortunately appears as if this is the case far too often. As explained by Joy (2010), our schemas evolve out of highly structured belief systems. These belief systems are sociological in nature, and may or may not be grounded in evidence. Once the schemas have been formed in the minds of those in question, regardless of whether or not they were created by a flawed belief system, it is through these schemas that future information obtained from interactions will be filtered. In this way, "not only do our beliefs ultimately lead to our actions, but our actions also reinforce our beliefs" (Joy, 2010, p. 16). This cycle gives schemas their strength and renders them static rather than fluid in nature.

Before I apply Joy's argument to ableism as well as speciesism, I would first like to clarify the definitions of a few critical terms as they pertain to this chapter. The first is the concept of disability, or how one comes to be labeled disabled:

> If one hears the term disability or disabled person or people with a disability... often two different aspects (body image and social reality) are covered by the term disability. If one would talk about the body in ability studies language one could use the term ability diverse (neutral language) or ability deficient (biased term). If one talks about the social disablement, the negative social reality, the social discrimination especially socially disadvantaged groups and people face, in ability studies language one could say ability expectation oppressed people or people impacted by ability expectations. (Wollbring, 2014, p. 2)

While both conceptualizations of disability are necessary in order to understand its complex social and persynal undertones along with its visible and invisible aspects, for the purposes of this chapter, the term "disabled" will be used to refer to those who are seen as lacking in a certain ability (whether this judgement is made by themselves or others). It will not be used to address the social and physical barriers which disable certain persyns, unless otherwise stated.

Another term which will play a vital role in this discussion is eco-ability. Ecoability, a movement recently constructed by Anthony J. Nocella II (2012), is akin to the term ecofeminism because it problematizes the concept of normalcy by exposing its true nature as a sociological construct. It "arose out of the animal advocacy, environmental, and disability rights movements to challenge dominance of normalcy, competition, and individualism" (Nocella, 2012, p. 2). In contrast to the current modern, patriarchal society which highly values individualism in addition to normalcy, those engaged with eco-ability theory cherish, and seek to encourage, the unique and the collective. It is this particular aspect of eco-ability, which promotes difference within interdependency that will be most relevant for this chapter.

Lastly, a phrase that is necessary to define is a system of oppression. For Joy (2010), a system can be viewed as oppressive when it, among other things, elicits what she has termed "The Cognitive Trio." For Joy (2010), "The Cognitive Trio" involves objectification, deindividualization, and dichotomization. As ecofeminist Carol Adams (1995) has stated, objectification is defined as when a persyn (whether humyn or nonhumyn) is viewed as a non-sentient object and is treated as such. Deindividualization, as defined by Joy (2010), is similar in that the persyn in question loses their individuality, their identity as a single, unique being, but are still regarded as a living. Although, their lived existence is only really acknowledged insofar as they are part of a group: "deindividualization is the process of viewing individuals only in terms of their group identity and as having the same characteristics as everyone else in the group. [It] is viewing others only as members of a whole" (Joy, 2010, p. 119). This is very similar to Adams' concept of the "mass term" which she describes as a "linguistic dance done around butchered animal flesh" (1995). She goes on to say, "We don't say a lamb's leg, we say leg of lamb. We take away the possessive relationship between a lamb and his or her leg. Animals are not mass terms. Water is a mass term" (Adams, 1995). For both Adams and Joy, whether it is the notion of mass terms or deindividualization which is being discussed, the result is that, in becoming a part of a certain group, individuals find themselves losing their individuality.

It is at this stage of the "Cognitive Trio," wherein the individual persyns are being grouped, that dichotomization plays a role. Dichotomization occurs during the particular form of categorization in which values are assigned, for example, when "disabled" is categorized as being of less value. It is a very common form of categorization, perhaps the most common form of social categorization, in which strict binaries are created, thus making the line between those who are valued, and those who are not, even thicker. It is these three psychological and social events which Joy (2010) claims make up "The Cognitive Trio," which she argues results in the normalized separation between certain groups, and the assumption that this separation is somehow based on naturally-assigned values of who matters and who does not. To put it simply, when a group of unique individuals is being considered with the "The Cognitive Trio" at work in the mind, though they are individuals, [they are] viewed as abstractions—as a "bunch" of things" (Joy, 2010, p. 116).

As a system of oppression, ableism follows the rule, so to speak, of "The Cognitive Trio" by promoting the objectification, deindividualization, and dichotomization of disabled persyns. This is accomplished through the existence of cultural ability preferences. The term "ability preferences" is a way of referring to the nearly universal phenomenon of certain "abilities" being viewed as more valuable and critical to the humyn experience than others (Wollbring, 2014). Two primary examples of such abilities are the capability to use rational thought and the capability to walk on two legs. This belief system, which prizes these two abilities (and related ones) in a hierarchal fashion above others, contributes to the formation of psychological schemas which are then used to sort persyns into groups based on their perceived capability to perform these tasks. This categorization is not inherently concerning, however, problems arise when certain categories are viewed as more valuable than others. This leads to the conclusion that the persyns belonging to these categories are more valuable than others, thus creating discriminative generalizations and oppressive ideologies. One of these oppressive ideologies is speciesism. The belief-system behind speciesism, and the way in which the discrimination towards various species is formulated and justified, is extremely similar to that of ableism. In general, "the exploitation of other animals and the justification of their mistreatment not only closely resemble human oppression but are inextricably tied to it" (Nibert, 2002, p. 3). At its most basic level, speciesism is the discriminative set of beliefs which maintains that the humyn species inherently holds more value than any other species. The speciesist mindset involves a strict hierarchy with certain animals (often species which are viewed as "companion species," such as dogs and cats) closer to the top; however, humyns are always placed in the topmost dominating position. At its foundation, as is the case with every discriminative ideology, speciesism is based on the idea that one group (the nonhumyn animals) are different from another (the humyn animals) in some way, which is inferred to mean that they are less valuable. More specifically, speciesism at its core holds the position that nonhumyn persyns are categorically different from humyn persyns due to their "inability" to perform certain tasks and actions. And just as is the case with ableism, two of these actions which are considered to be of particular importance when it comes to this categorization are that of being able to think rationally and walk bipedally (on two legs).

Nowhere are the consequences of speciesist oppression more obvious than within the animal agriculture industry. This industry, could not exist were it not for the extreme objectification and de-individualization of non-humyn animals. Fish, chickens, pigs, goats, sheep, turkeys, rabbits, cows, and other species are killed by the trillions every single year. Tragically, the fact that such an unimaginably large number of these persyns are slaughtered annually only works to further their oppression. For the larger a group becomes, and the more distanced one feels from said group (and the more innate one believes this separation to be), the less compassionate one will feel for that group. The psychologist Paul Slovic discovered this when he spent time studying the relationship between the number of victims in a traumatic situation and the reaction of the witnesses. He found that, if a tragedy had a large number of victims, witnesses more frequently depersonalized them and appeared less emotionally affected by their suffering. He also noted that this process of "psychic numbing," as he labeled it, would commence after the group became larger than just two people. His final realization was that, "numbers and numbing go hand in hand. The death of one person is a tragedy; the death of a group is a statistic" (Slovic, 2007, p. 94). To summarize, unlike groupings of objectified, de-individualized persyns lumped into an oppressive single category, individuals are far more likely to elicit sympathy/arouse compassion.

While knowing that we humyns often act in a way that appears so callous can be distressing, having such information is literally invaluable for those who wish to alter this reality—a reality which involves a dangerously problematic over-reliance on schemas and generalizations which in turn leads to discrimination, violence, and oppression. Understanding the social and psychological mechanisms involved in the formation of oppressive mindsets and apathetic attitudes means that social justice activists who are fighting for the rights of the oppressed, can be more strategic, and therefore more effective with the methods they use to elicit social change. The method that will be the primary focus here is the act of "bearing witness," with an emphasis on the integration of feminist care techniques. To begin with an anecdotal example of the power of bearing witness, I would like to use the story of Emily the cow; a persyn who escaped from a slaughterhouse in Massachusetts. After evading those the slaughterhouse had tasked with capturing her, a feat that she accomplished partially because she was aided by people in the community who became emotionally invested in her plight, she finally found a safe, permanent home where she received love and care. Shortly after her death (of natural causes), a memorial was held, during which one of the attendants expressed how Emily's life had catalyzed a new awareness in people. The attendee of the memorial explained how Emily's large, luminous brown eyes communicated so much more than words ever could and how such connections gave wordless testimony to the urgent necessity for an all-embracing compassion. This example demonstrates the immense power of giving attention to the stories of the oppressed and silenced through bearing witness. Bearing witness is about facing the suffering of an individual directly, even when it would be easier to turn away, and helping them in whatever way possible, even if that way is just by being present. Toronto Pig, Cow, and Chicken Saves are animal rights sister organizations, of which I am a member and co-founder. They exist under the global umbrella of "The Save Movement" a global activist collective which was created when Save groups began being organized in other cities and countries. The purpose of The Toronto Save groups is to bear witness to the tens of thousands of nonhumyn animals who are killed each day in slaughterhouses in and around Toronto. The activists interact with the animals directly as they wait, trapped in filthy, metal transport trucks, to be forcibly unloaded into the place of their violent deaths. These interactions happen during weekly "vigils" and consist of everything from providing water, to giving a gentle, loving caress. In photojournalist Jo-Anne McArthur's interview with Anita Krajnc, one of the co-founders of Toronto Pig Save and The Save Movement, Krajnc states that her inspiration came from the following quote from Leo Tolstoy's *A Calendar of Wisdom*: "When the suffering of another creature causes you to feel pain, do not submit to the initial desire to flee from the suffering one, but on the contrary, come closer, as close as you can to him who suffers, and try to help" (Tolstoy, 1910/2017). Put into practice, Krajnc explains/argues, that this requires one to see, listen to, and touch the persyns being transported to slaughter, who are purposely sequestered and silenced in invisible (and unimaginable) places (Krajnc, 2012). Krajnc makes it clear that bearing witness is far more involved than mere "witnessing" on its own. When one participates in a vigil, one's senses are bombarded with the same smells, sounds, and sights as the animals. This alone is jarring and forces the humyn persyn to begin understanding what the animal persyns in the trucks in front of them must be experiencing. This understanding only deepens as one gets closer to the truck. One may hear their sporadic cries and the panicked shuffling of their feet, occasionally interspersed with a thud as one of the individuals trips over another. One may see their eyes bulging with fear or tearing up with despair. One may even feel their emotional experiences through touch as many of them will seek the comfort of a gentle caress. By engaging with the animals in this way, whether through the use of one of the senses or them all, one is made aware of the individuality of the animal, who they may have previously thought of as only an objectified member of a category. As a result of this new awareness, the humyn persyn may very likely alter their ethical guidelines by which they live their life. The idea of living in an ethical manner as a result of such emotional interactions is what ecofeminists call the "ethics of care." Josephine Donovan describes the ethics of care as the following:

> A recognition of their subjecthood [which] not only engenders ethical knowledge; that ethical knowledge, it is here claimed, *inheres in* and *emerges from* the communicative encounter between subjects. There is, in short, an ethical substrate—a cosmic sympathy, expressed through what I am calling *emotional qualia* that comes alive or becomes apparent in communicative encounters between living entities. Just as qualitative properties, such as taste, smell, or feel of a physical entity arise or emerge when a subject encounter that object, so emotional qualia emerge in one's encounter with another subject. (Donovan, 2014, p. 76)

For Donovan and other ecofeminists such as myself, the ethical consciousness which arises through an interaction of two persyns whose subjective lived stories have become intertwined is tangible, and is in every way as valid as knowledge obtained via modern, scientific techniques, if not more so. Indeed, upon consideration of the positive social changes that would likely arise through the mass dissemination of such ethical knowledge, the act of bearing witness becomes revolutionary for both the individual and the collective.

Here, I would like to briefly return to the passage at the very beginning. Usually, at Toronto Cow Save vigils, we unfortunately only have a few minutes with the animals, but, on this day, I spent over fifteen with this one individual persyn. Despite having been to countless vigils before, I was still shocked by the emotional strength of the connection which took form during our communication; the connection which saw me being dragged away from the truck by a fellow activist when I could not physically make myself leave his side, not even when the truck started moving. In hindsight, I believe that it was my experience of Donovan's "cosmic sympathy" that is responsible for my particular desperation to save him at that moment. Through the sound of his anguished and panicked bellows and the sight of his pain, a sense of ethical responsibility made it into my ears and into my soul. It is events such as these that make bearing witness so powerful. Even though my particular story of bearing witness centers around my intersubjective emotional experience with a nonhumyn persyn, this understanding of ethical responsibility arising naturally through moments of bearing witness applies to any interaction between two subjects. For example, one could apply these exact principles to bearing witness with those who are disabled and are experiencing homelessness, a population of humyn persyns whose existence, and certainly their individual subjectivities and stories, are also hidden away and ignored.

In conclusion, it has been put forth in this chapter that the basis for oppressive systems such as ableism and speciesism is both psychological and sociological in nature, as they involve the formation of mental schemas, which are founded on, and in turn encourage and strengthen, potentially problematic social generalizations and belief systems. One such belief system is that the ability to form rational thought, as well as the ability to stand bipedally, are of the utmost importance. As such, those who are viewed as not being capable of accomplishing these two over-valued actions, such as persyns with disabilities and nonhumyn persyns, find themselves being categorized within an ableist binary system. Once in this system, these individuals are now viewed as "other" and "less valuable" and have their identities as unique persyns with their own subjectivities and stories stripped away. Once they become viewed as this grouping of "other somethings," atrocities which are done unto them are viewed as less deserving of a compassionate reaction than if the same had been done to an individual whose unique subjectivity was recognized and valued. The act of bearing witness was discussed as having the power to bring awareness to the subjective experiences and stories of those who have been objectified and silenced by speciesist and ableist rhetoric. It accomplishes this by encouraging intense sensory and emotional interactions between persyns who would not otherwise communicate. These interactions give rise to a collective ethical consciousness which is an invaluable form of knowledge that can only be obtained through emotional and so-called "irrational" means. Because eco-ability rejects the glorification of independence and modern intellectualism, which holds the belief that knowledge may only be obtained through rational scientific means, bearing witness can be defined as a form of radical eco-ability activism. Both eco-ability and bearing witness place emphasis on the recognition of the critical importance of creating a collective through the recognition and validation of unique differences, and so it could be said that the two go hand-in-hand in fighting oppression. To put it plainly and simply, the remarkable subversive power of eco-ability theory and the act of bearing witness is in their ability to put a face to the nameless numbers.

References

Adams, C. (1995). *Do feminists need to liberate animals too?* Retrieved from http://carol jadams.com/new-page-2/

Donovan, J. (2014). Participatory epistemology, sympathy, and animal ethics. In C. J. Adams & L. Gruen (Eds.), *Ecofeminism. Feminists intersections with other animals & the earth* (pp. 75–90). New York, NY: Bloomsbury Academic.

Joy, M. (2010). *Why we love dogs eat pigs and wear cows.* San Francisco, CA: Conari Press.

Krajnc, A. (2012). *Bearing witness: A guest blog by Anita Krajnc, co-founder of Toronto Pig Save*. Jo-Anne McArthur We Animals. Retrieved from http://weanimals.org/blog.php?entry=168

Nibert, D. (2002). *Animal rights, human rights. Entanglements of oppression and liberation*. Lanham, MD: Rowman & Littlefield Publishers.

Nocella, A. J. (2012). Defining eco-ability: Social justice and the intersectionality of disability, nonhuman animals, and ecology. In A. J. Nocella, C. K. Bently, & J. M. Duncan (Eds.), *Earth, animal, and disability liberation: The rise of the eco-ability movement* (pp. 1–21). New York, NY: Peter Lang Publishing.

Slovic, P. (2007). "If I look at the mass I will never act": Psychic numbing and genocide. *Judgment and Decision Making, 2*(2), 79–95.

Tolstoy, L. (1910/2017). *Calendar of wisdom*. Richmond, UK: Alma Books.

Wollbring, G. (2014). *Ability studies: A field to analyze social justice issues and identities of humans, animals, and nature*. Retrieved from http://www.ucalgary.ca/uofc/Others/CRDS/research/faculty/criticaljunctiontalk3.pdf

7. Reframing Companion Animal Disability Using the Social Model: Removing Barriers and Facilitating Care

Nicole R. Pallotta

Companion animal disability can be viewed through multiple lenses but any analysis must take into account the fact that animals are strictly defined as property under the law and thus do not possess legal rights (Favre, 2010; Francione, 2004; Frasch, Katherine Hessler, Kutil, & Waisman, 2011; Huss, 2002; Sunstein & Nussbaum, 2005; Waisman, Frasch, & Wagman, 2014; Wise, 2000). While there are parallels with human disability, their property status places animals with disabilities in an uniquely vulnerable positon, as they are at the mercy of a human owner who has complete control over the animal's life, provided their behavior does not cross the threshold into criminal animal cruelty or neglect (and even then, enforcement of such laws is a perennial problem [Waisman et al., 2014, p. 75]). The best parallel may be to children with disabilities because they too are legally and socially dependent on an adult to meet their needs and provide care, but an animal's status as property renders this analogy incomplete.

Taking into account the sociological confines of property status, but assuming guardians have a respectful and loving relationship with their companion animal, and are committed to providing the best care leading to an excellent quality of life, there are improvements that could be made to remove systemic barriers that impede animals with disabilities from receiving quality assistance. The underpinning of this analysis rests on the framework that companion animals have intrinsic value and an inherent right to life, coupled with adopting the social model of understanding disability. I will use my personal experience caring for a disabled canine family member to examine broader social issues that impact access and care.

Thinking about Disability

Until the 1980s, disability was typically analyzed using a medical model, which focuses on understanding disability or illness from a clinical perspective in which health care providers and medical knowledge are central. Under the medical model, disability is viewed as a problem that exists in a person's body. However, in recent decades a social model that focuses on societal aspects of disability—specifically the ways access to mainstream society is restricted for individuals with impairments—has gained prominence in the field as a more accurate way to capture the experience of "disability." The social model distinguishes between impairment and disability, with the latter resulting from being excluded from the social environment (Moyne, 2012). It is this lack of access that defines disability, rather than the particulars of a medical diagnosis. The social model thus focuses on aspects of social organization that engender differential treatment and act as barriers to mainstream society, rather than on the clinical factors of the individual's impairment, in an effort to better understand the experience of living with a disability (Goering, 2015; Morris, 2001; Oliver, 1996).

When my dog Alec became paralyzed, our world changed profoundly and we both experienced new challenges. In thinking about companion animal disability, we might use a medical or individualistic model to inquire 1) how the impairment affects the individual animal emotionally and physically (this includes questions relating to happiness, quality of life, and pain management) and, 2) how it affects the caretaker's life, an experience that will be framed in part by the caretaker's beliefs and attitudes, and the meaning they have ascribed to their relationship with the individual animal. Using the medical model, we might also focus on the veterinary medical establishment and the current state of medicine and clinical knowledge about various disabilities affecting animals, including surgical options, medical and diagnostic procedures, prosthetics, physical therapy, and other therapeutic modalities. All of these questions were central to my experience caring for Alec, but issues of social structure equally affected the circumstances that shaped our lives as we navigated our "new normal."

There is some overlap with questions framed using a medical versus social lens, but the latter's focus on "disability" as an issue of equal access to mainstream society—arising not from individual impairment or limited function but from aspects of social organization that act as barriers—can help us think about companion animal disability in expanded ways.

The Cultural Mythology of "Unconditional Love"

My love for Alec was boundless, igniting both powerful emotion and practical action. I would have done anything for him, and was happy to reshape my life after he became paralyzed to meet his new needs. I believe our bond was mutual, but I am only comfortable using the phrase "unconditional love" to describe my own feelings. Indeed, one of my pet peeves, so to speak, is the concept of unconditional love as attributed to dogs by humans.

Although a well-intentioned way to romanticize dogs, it is both overused and misused in the context of human-canine relations. Particularly problematic is the tacit expectation that unconditional love flows in one direction only—from dogs to us. Despite the cultural belief that dogs possess this ability as an inherent trait, we rarely flip the script and ask about our own willingness to love a vulnerable animal in this boundless way. And it bears repeating that animals—classified as property in an anthropocentric, hierarchical society—are always vulnerable. Leaving aside questions of what kind of emotions nonhuman animals experience, a critical look at the cultural ideal of unconditional love as applied by the dominant species (humans) to a subordinate one (domesticated dogs) in American culture reveals several problems. Perhaps most importantly, it rather conveniently obscures power dynamics.

Dogs in American society are utterly dependent upon their owners (despite the increasing popularity of the word "guardian," this term is not backed by law) for everything, from basic necessities like food, water, and shelter to higher order social and psychological needs like companionship, exercise, and mental stimulation. In this way, they are similar to children, who cannot choose the parents that until a certain age will constitute their whole world and may be wonderful or horrible; as a result, children may continue to love parents who abuse and neglect them.

Unconditional love takes on a twisted and tragic meaning in this and similar contexts where it is built upon a foundation of pronounced power imbalance. In a relationship where one party has complete control, the concept of unconditional love becomes a facet of the dominant ideology that serves to legitimize and mask power relations inherent in the dog-human relationship. Although an increasing number of Americans identify their companion animals as family members (Grimm, 2014), this is very much a provisional status, which can be terminated at will by the member of the relationship who is not legally defined as property, and therefore has the absolute authority to define (and subsequently redefine) the relationship.

Although they indisputably occupy a more privileged cultural position than, for example, farmed animals, society harbors contradictory values about companion animals. It is still legal to buy and sell them, reinforcing a social status more akin to commodities than family members. It is also legal and socially acceptable to terminate the fictive "family member" relationship at any time. In the U.S., countless healthy dogs are relinquished to shelters each year, approximately half of whom are killed (ASPCA, 2016), for trivial reasons that would be considered nonsensical if applied to a human family member. It is impossible to know if everyone who gives up their dog for lifestyle reasons (unwillingness to devote time, energy, or financial resources to caring for the animal) claimed in happier times that their dog loved them unconditionally, but it is likely in a society in which this cultural narrative is prominent.

In this cultural climate, having a disability places vulnerable companion animals in an even more precarious position. Attitudes are one of the most significant barriers to inclusion in mainstream society both for people (Anderson, 2012) and animals with disabilities; for animals they also mean life or death in terms of whether an owner decides to accommodate the disability or "euthanize" their pet. Cultural attitudes and social norms about what is acceptable treatment of companion animals is an important and fundamental aspect of applying the social model to animals with disabilities.

Yet, the U.S. legal system's designation of animals as personal property does not reflect the lived experience of the growing number of Americans who have defined their relationships with their companion animals differently (Shannon-Missal, 2015). Despite the broader socio-legal context in which corporations, ships, and cities can be "legal persons" but animals are "legal things" (Dyschkant, 2015; Huss, 2002; Prosin & Wise, 2014), at the micro level many people cherish the companion animals with whom they share their lives and are devoted to their well-being.

Alec's Story

My rescued German shepherd Alec was the love of my life. First and foremost, he was a unique and special individual in his own right. In relation to me, Alec was my best friend, constant companion, and treasured family member. I loved him beyond words. We had been together five wonderful, happy years when Alec suddenly developed rear limb paralysis at age seven due to acute intervertebral disk disease. After a routine trip to the park to play he began limping and by the time we got to the vet, less than an hour later, he could no longer walk. After two emergency spinal cord surgeries, life-threatening complications, and twelve days hospitalized at a specialty veterinary facility, Alec remained paralyzed, lacking even the ability to urinate on his own.

Given the severity of the situation, I was told he might not live. But he did. The fact that Alec was alive was all that mattered to me, but he now had serious medical needs. One of the first things I needed to learn was how to manually express his bladder, which involves locating the bladder with your hands and squeezing very hard until you can push all of the urine out. It was incredibly difficult for both of us, but extremely important because if I did not completely vacate his bladder multiple times a day, Alec would quickly develop an infection.

At 70 pounds, Alec's size made my daunting new nursing duties more difficult than they would have been with a smaller dog. I was terrified when he was discharged into my care and out of the hands of the trained technicians who had been caring for him around the clock at the animal hospital. Our lives had changed irrevocably and I honestly did not know—given Alec's size and the severity of his new medical needs—if I could care for him by myself.

To complicate matters further, we found ourselves without a place to live. After he was released from the veterinary hospital, I could not bring Alec home because the rental house where we had been living was only accessible by stairs, which in our new reality represented an insurmountable barrier. Having recently moved across the country, I had no family and few friends in the area. We had nowhere to go. Fortunately, the director of the animal protection organization where I was working allowed me to move into a vacant first-floor office while Alec recovered from surgery and I looked for new housing. Although it was strange to live in my office, I was immensely grateful to have a place to stay as Alec and I together faced an uncertain future.

Those first few weeks after Alec became paralyzed were characterized by continual stress and intermittent panic, but I did my best to maintain a positive attitude. When I couldn't hold it together after trying and trying to find his bladder but not succeeding, when my wrists were so sore I thought they were going to break from pressing on his abdomen (Alec could not feel this pressure), after struggling to keep him lying still on his side for this necessary indignity, and worrying my failure to vacate his bladder was going to create an infection and cause further complications for him, I would leave the office to quietly sob in the hallway so Alec wouldn't see me break down.

I struggled with feeling overwhelmed and scared, but I was so grateful he was alive. Most important to me was his emotional state, and I was keenly attuned to Alec's quality of life in the aftermath of losing his ability to walk. During this time, I monitored him closely for signs of depression, but I was amazed at Alec's resilience and cheerful demeanor in the face of these new challenges. Dogs seem to experience time differently than humans, privileging the present moment over worrying about the future or dwelling on the past (Bradshaw, 2011). This here-and-now focus may be beneficial in helping dogs adapt to disability and changed circumstances.

We lived in my office for almost two months while Alec recuperated from his surgeries and I learned to care for him. I slept on an air mattress, ate vegan microwave dinners, and developed a new routine with Alec that involved gentle physical therapy (which at this point was mainly light massage and passive range of motion), helping Alec to rotate his position so he would not develop pressure sores, the dreaded but necessary bladder expression every four to six hours, and constantly cleaning soiled beds—and Alec himself—with a waterless shampoo. Keeping his body and bedding clean was an ongoing challenge because he could no longer control his bowel movements, nor get up to avoid them, and would dribble urine between the times when I expressed his bladder. Before moving into our office, I had visited the local thrift store to stock up on pillows, blankets, and sheets, which we went through rapidly. My friends and coworkers hauled large bags full of soiled bedding home with them every other night to launder for me so that Alec would have clean bedding. They also kindly donated packages of wee-wee pads and other necessary supplies, the cost of which quickly added up. I left Alec's side only to dash to the bathroom, and occasionally take makeshift "showers" standing on a towel hovered over the industrial sink in the supply closet. Alec had his own sleeping area, but one night he dragged himself over to my air mattress, and after that we slept together side by side on the tiny bed. He took up most of the mattress but I didn't dare try to move him and risk hurting his back, which was still healing after surgery, so I ended up partway on the floor each night. I did not mind.

We returned to the veterinary hospital for rechecks after Alec's surgeries, and after the sixth week when his "deep pain sensation" (DPP)—essentially a way to measure nerve function by determining if he had any feeling in his paralyzed limbs—still had not returned, the neurologists gave him a "poor prognosis for return to normal function," meaning he would never walk again. My heart sank as I worried what the future would hold, but Alec was alive, had the same personality, and was happy, which again was all that mattered to me. In the interim, although I had hoped he could recover, I researched dogs living with paralysis (having almost no previous knowledge of the subject) and found that even big dogs could successfully use a mobility cart, or "dog wheelchair," to get around.

So I ordered him a mobility cart and tried to learn everything I could about taking care of a large dog with hind end paralysis. As long as Alec could have a good quality of life using his wheelchair, which I was satisfied he could after doing my research, I would do everything in my power to ensure his happiness, including rearranging my life to accommodate his new medical needs. I was glad to do it, but the fear that I might not be able to physically care for him remained. I started having back problems myself during this time from the strain of handling and lifting him. If my back went out, what would happen to us? But we made it work, with the help of some generous friends and a compassionate local veterinarian who made "house" calls to my office to check on Alec every couple days to make sure I was emptying his bladder sufficiently. That process was still difficult, but I was getting better at it. After two months we moved out of my office and into a new rental home with the help of a friend who built a wonderful hinged ramp for Alec to get in and out of the house, enabling him to pass over the front steps. (In caring for Alec, I noticed for the first time how many structures have stairs, and how many curbs at street corners do not have ramps, essentially making them steps.)

That first year was an amazing journey filled with unexpected milestones. I continued to perform regular physical therapy with Alec, and despite that poor prognosis, he began to slowly but steadily improve. His bladder function returned first. Bladder expression was easily the most challenging thing for both of us (and was one aspect of the disability that I believe did negatively affect his quality of life), so after that everything else was a bonus. One day I walked into the room and the tip of his tail, which had been paralyzed along with his rear legs, wagged, just for a moment, the way it used to when he saw me. I thought I would never see him wag his tail again and I rejoiced at this small movement. I bought him a life vest and began taking him to the river for hydrotherapy. To my delight and amazement, his back legs actually moved a little in the water. We also did sessions in an underwater treadmill at a canine rehabilitation center and other forms of physical therapy at home, such as weight-bearing and supported standing. Because of his size and my difficulty holding his weight, the mobility cart aided greatly with these rehab exercises.

Alec adjusted easily to his cart and enjoyed being able to go on walks again. When I put him in the cart, I placed his back legs in little suspenders that held his paws off the ground so they wouldn't drag. As we walked, I eventually noticed his back legs moving slightly in the stirrups—just a little movement at first, so small I wasn't sure I was really seeing it, but gradually they were moving more and more.

Five months after he became paralyzed, Alec stood up on his own for the first time. I walked into my bedroom and saw him standing on the air mattress and shrieked with delight and ran to get my camera. That first time was brief—maybe ten seconds before he wobbled and fell over—but over time he started to stand for longer periods of time, until he began taking one or two baby steps. He continued to make slow and steady progress until almost a year later Alec took his first walk around the block without his wheelchair. After this milestone, we still used the mobility cart but I was able to gradually extend his time outside of it until he no longer needed it.

Alec still had distinct needs and a level of disability. Because his right hind leg was not fully functional, he walked with a limp that caused his foot to drag. He had to wear a special shoe to protect his paw on hard surfaces. And because he would always be at risk of reinjuring his back, he was not supposed to run, jump, or wrestle with other dogs. He would always need to avoid stairs.

Life was more complicated (although nothing like those first months after surgery) but that was okay. Alec still had a full life. Even though he could no longer run around on land, I was able to make it up to him with regular swimming, where he could engage in his favorite activity (fetch!) in the relative safety of water. Alec loved to swim and I was grateful for this because swimming became an important physical and psychological outlet given his restrictions on solid ground. I devoted time to searching for accessible swimming spots. We swam in calm rivers, lakes, and indoor pools, and continued our weekly hydrotherapy sessions in an underwater treadmill. I also sought out flat, grassy places where he could walk safely without his shoe. We continued with the physical therapy, not knowing when he would hit a "wall" in terms of improvement. It wasn't until two and a half years after his spinal cord operations that Alec finally reached a plateau. Although he had a limp, contrary to the prognosis given to us by the neurologists, he was walking.

I started a personal blog during this time to keep family and friends updated about our situation, and an unexpected consequence of reporting on Alec's rehabilitation was that guardians with dogs in similar situations found us and reached out to say we had given them hope. It is important to emphasize that not every dog in Alec's situation will walk again, but it is equally important to not give up too soon based on incomplete information if any measure of improvement affecting quality of life is possible. Through my experience with Alec, I learned there is much that is unknown about neurological injuries.

When I started my blog, I was scared but trying to maintain hope. Writing about our experience was a way for me to manage my fear and uncertainty. I had no idea that so many people would write to me to tell me that our story had given them hope when their own dog became paralyzed. I cried tears of joy when I heard from strangers that Alec's story had inspired them to not give up on their disabled animal companions.

Although my story is about a dog who did walk again, our experience is also relevant in cases where that will not happen. Even if Alec had never walked again, the physical therapy we did was important because it strengthened his core muscles, which supported his back and helped keep him strong. Swimming was important for physical conditioning as well as psychological stimulation that movement and play brought to him.

Inherent Value

After Alec developed paralysis, I learned it was not uncommon for people to euthanize dogs with a similar prognosis. Although my friends and family understood my wholehearted commitment to Alec, there is not a cultural consensus on the value of a pet's life. My housemate at the time told a friend of hers what was happening when Alec was still hospitalized, and he responded saying that a bullet would have been less expensive. Although I was appalled by this person's comment, I know the callous disregard and utilitarian way of thinking about animals it represented is not completely aberrant in a culture that views dogs as disposable.

Even if an owner is willing to do whatever it takes to give her animal a good quality of life after developing a disability, she may face subtle and not-so-subtle resistance from those in whom she must now place her faith and trust: veterinary professionals. Not only was I given no hope by the veterinary neurologists that Alec would walk again, but one vet in particular was actively discouraging and questioned my decision (and ability) to care for him despite his life-changing condition.

My devotion to Alec carried me through the dark times, but for others who do not have such a close bond with their dog, such a prognosis could easily tip them to a decision to put their dog to death (I have serious qualms about the word "euthanasia" when it is a done for the convenience and comfort of the owner rather than mercy for an animal who is suffering). When Alec received that poor prognosis, I did my best to research his condition on my own. However, I soon discovered there was very little long-term data on large dogs with his type of injury. This dearth of data results in part from the fact that when they are given no hope by their veterinarian, or information about responsible and supportive caretaking in light of a permanent but not life-threatening impairment, many caretakers are left thinking euthanasia is the only feasible option.

As I tried to navigate my new role as caretaker of a large dog who had suddenly acquired a disability, it was not easy to work with some of the veterinarians' pessimism, and at times the dismissive attitudes were dismaying to say the least. Reflecting on the trying experiences, I am grateful for the staff who were more supportive and, while being careful not to diminish the severity of the diagnosis, did tell me they had seen amazing things happen with physical therapy in some individual cases (though of course not all). In a vast of sea of what seemed to be indifference to Alec's life, this was all the encouragement I needed and I am so grateful I did not listen to the first neurologist.

Whether or not he walked again, Alec was able to enjoy a good quality of life, and the fact that a respected veterinary neurologist in a state-of-the-art animal care facility was so thoroughly discouraging in response to my willingness to do everything I could for Alec raises the question: how many other guardians in similar situations are given a message by trusted veterinary professionals that suggest it will be impossible for them to manage their dog's care on their own or that physical therapy is a waste of time—essentially giving them no hope and steering them toward a decision to euthanize their newly disabled animal? I don't want to sugarcoat my experience caring for Alec; it was very difficult. But every step was worth it, and would have been even if he never walked again. The fact that he did suggests there could be countless dogs in similar situations who are never given the chance, either due to caretakers who decline to put forth the effort or added expense to care for a disabled animal, or are discouraged by veterinary professionals from giving their animal a chance to live with his or her disability.

I was able to uncover one single study when I tried to research Alec's condition on my own, a research report published in the *Journal of the American Veterinary Medical Association*, which revealed that "persistent absence of DPP does not necessarily indicate that a dog will be persistently paraplegic. The development of a voluntary tail wag was a useful early prognostic sign for recovery of motor function in such dogs" (Olby et al., 2003, p. 768). It also noted that in the 70 case studies of dogs with conditions like Alec's, 17% were euthanized at their owner's request: six of these dogs were euthanized upon initial examination (the owner opted not to do surgery), two dogs were euthanized three weeks after surgery due to lack of improvement, and four were euthanized two, four, nine, and 36 months after surgery due to lack of improvement.

This was the only study I could track down that dealt with Alec's condition, and it was not easy to find. I am glad I was able to locate it because the research finding about an early tail wag being a good prognostic indicator gave me hope, and indeed this small sign did end up being a harbinger of further improvements and return of motor function. But I had to discover this on my own. In the absence of significant longitudinal data, messages given to clients by the veterinary establishment should be appropriately measured. Attitudes like the one I encountered from the first neurologist, dissuading me not only from trying physical therapy but also attempting to care for Alec at all, undoubtedly contribute to inflated euthanasia rates of disabled animals and perpetuate a lack of long-term data that would more accurately predict recovery rates and outcomes for dogs who do not recover.

Finally, a widely held misconception about animals who become disabled is that they cannot enjoy a high quality of life; this is a myth (Taylor, 2014). While it is true that an owner may perceive the extra of time and effort needed to care for the animal as an increased burden, disabled animals like Alec can and do enjoy their lives. Evidence suggests that dogs do not dwell on the fact that yesterday they could run and today they cannot; they focus on the present moment (Bradshaw, 2011), and with the assistance of a caring and informed guardian they can make a relatively smooth adjustment to their new reality. In the study cited above, even owners of dogs who retained some amount of incontinence and had a lengthy recovery reported their animal was "happy and functional," and that they were pleased with their dogs' quality of life.

Although Alec's physical abilities were altered, his demeanor never changed. With the adjustments we made, including the mobility cart and new swimming routine, his quality of life remained high and his attitude stayed joyful and enthusiastic. He was a happy dog, always. I will note that caring for an animal with paraplegia and trying to aid their recovery and or/adaptation to the impairment through rehabilitation can be expensive, as with all veterinary care. I paid several hundred dollars for the mobility cart, surgery costs are astronomical (I charged thousands of dollars across multiple credit cards to pay the discharge bill after Alec's hospitalization and operations), and underwater treadmill sessions are expensive, as are consultations with veterinary rehabilitation specialists. However, the aid of rehabilitation professionals is important. Without proper guidance you could easily injure your animal. For example, you should never take a dog who has paraplegia into a river without professional advice relating to your dog's particular medical condition. But there is an increasing number of resources available for caretakers of disabled dogs and as awareness grows, and more information is gained about neurological injuries in both people and animals, there is cause to hope for improved outcomes in the future.

I want to again stress that although it was central to our experience and the story of our lives together, the main point of this essay is not that Alec regained his ability to walk, but rather to point out the barriers that exist for caretakers of dogs who become disabled in ways similar to Alec. Many dogs with acute intervertebral disk disease do walk again, sometimes in a matter of days or weeks; others end up with a permanent impairment. Of course after being told he would never walk again I wondered how many other guardians had received erroneous dim prognoses. But the larger point is that animals with disabilities have lives that matter, can enjoy a good quality of life even if their impairment remains unchanged (in cases like Alec's—I cannot speak to all conditions of course), and deserve support that will enable them to thrive.

Removing Barriers and Facilitating Care

The most immediate barrier to a good quality of life for animals with disabilities is at the same time both personal and societal: the owner's devotion and willingness to provide care for their companion animal. While this potential barrier is literally an individual (or family), it is also extra-personal because as a matter of social structure and law the owner is given complete discretion over how to deal (or not deal) with her pet's disability (as would not be the case with a child, for example). However, beyond the fixed macro aspects (legal status of "owner") and more fluid micro aspects (how each individual acts and interprets that status) of the role of the owner, there are additional structural barriers and social constraints that are external to the owner-pet relationship that could be improved with more available resources and social acceptance of disability.

Proponents of the social model of disability are critical of the medical model's emphasis on finding a cure or "fixing" an impaired individual. However, depending on the nature of the disability it is natural to hope for and exhaust possible options for recovery or return to a previous level of function. This is especially true in the field of veterinary neurology where information regarding probabilities and outcomes appears to be incomplete—likely in part due to the premature euthanasia of dogs with hind leg paralysis, which thus leads to a reduced sample and skewed data about improvement potentialities and may create a self-perpetuating cycle. It would be disingenuous to claim that a dog would not prefer to be able to walk, run, wag her tail, and control her urination and defecation. Although now prominent in the field of disability studies, the social model has been challenged for its single-handed focus on disability as social in nature (Owens, 2015; Taylor, 2005; Terzi, 2004). Some have argued for a reconnection of the social concept of disability with the medical concept of impairment to reach a more complete and accurate understanding of the lived experience of those with disabilities, who may feel criticized for seeking a cure in cases where one may be possible (Shakespeare & Watson, 2002). When to accept an impairment and stop seeking a medical "solution" is a highly personal decision that will be navigated differently by each individual in accordance with many factors, including the nature of the impairment and available resources. In the case of an impairment that is permanent or chronic, the social model has much to offer by emphasizing every effort must be made to remove barriers in the social environment that transform an impairment into a disability.

For guardians of dogs who have become paralyzed, there are certain facets of social organization that could be improved in order to: 1) facilitate caretaking and make it less difficult (despite how distasteful it may seem to imagine an individual's disability being a burden for others, this barrier can be a reason for euthanasia of animals who develop paralysis) and, 2) maintain and enhance the animal's quality of life. Some of the following recommendations mirror social reforms that could be implemented to support the human-companion animal bond in society generally; these reforms could reduce the killing of unhoused animals, many of whom are relinquished to shelter facilities by their owners for reasons that could be addressed and alleviated at the policy level, for example banning no-pets clauses in rental housing and allowing companion animals on public transportation (Pallotta, 2016). Companion animals are already restricted from many public and private spaces in society, but for animals with disabilities like Alec's, and by extension their caretakers, the restrictions are even more pervasive and, as with people with disabilities, primarily related to access.

Accessible Rental Housing

The first step in reducing barriers to responsible care is increased access to rental housing for those who share their lives with companion animals, whether disabled or not. Specifically, blanket "no pets" restrictions (especially those based on size, breed, or other arbitrary criteria) should be banned and replaced with non-discriminatory policies that could still require references and deposits to cover potential damages but would ultimately base the decision to rent on information about the individual caretaker and her particular animal(s). Evictions would be allowed in cases of nuisance/noise disturbance, property damage, or if the animal is dangerous, but not for the mere fact of owning a pet. Ontario currently bans no-pet clauses and lobbying efforts are underway to institute similar legislation in Vancouver, B.C. (Larsen, 2016).

For those who don't own their own home, caring for a disabled animal can bring extra complications due to the fact that much rental housing prohibits pets altogether, or charges an extra fee when they are allowed. This severely restricts housing choices, and within the limited universe of available housing that allows companion animals, an even smaller subset of options will be accessible for a dog with impaired mobility. I was fortunate I had a landlord who allowed me to install a temporary ramp on the front porch, and a friend with the skills to construct it. Eventually I relocated to a less expensive city and found a first-floor apartment with only a small step up to the front door, carpet so Alec would not slip, and access to a level grassy outdoor area.

People with disabilities have protections under the Americans with Disabilities Act (ADA) when seeking a rental living space; landlords must make reasonable accommodations for a tenant with a disability at their own expense, and must allow the renter to make reasonable modifications to a unit to ensure safe and comfortable living conditions (Stewart, n.d.). Despite problems that may exist with implementation and enforcement of the ADA (Civil Rights Division of the U.S. Department of Justice, 2006), there is no such requirement for animals. Caretakers of companion animal with disabilities are on their own when seeking accessible rental housing; they must rely on personal resources alone since there is no social policy or law protecting companion animals with disabilities (or their owners). Elevating the legal status of animals beyond the category of personal property is likely a necessary first step to securing any rights in this area for them (even if, as is most likely, those rights would flow through their owner or guardian).

Accessible Exercise Areas

Despite the expansion of dog parks in recent years (El Nasser, 2001; Horn, 2015), many are not feasible recreation spaces for dogs with physical impairments like Alec's. A concentration of many animals in a small space (a feature of many dog parks) is problematic for dogs with impairments that put them at risk if confronted with rowdy dogs with varying levels of socialization skills who will engage in rough play. Further, Alec's movement was very circumscribed on land following his developing paraplegia, and swimming become an essential activity. One lake in particular had characteristics that worked well for him (e.g., sandy and level shore without a steep drop-off), but only allowed dogs access during six months of the year, so I could not bring Alec in the warmer months when the area was also being used by people. We eventually discovered an indoor canine pool facility where Alec could swim regularly, which was a blessing for us but it was not cheap. We were fortunate to be given a discount due to the owner's compassion about our situation.

After he became disabled, some of my happiest moments consisted of seeing Alec tired and content after a swim session, where he would chase after his ball in the water and enjoy a physically and mentally stimulating aquatic workout. It is a positive sign that more of these facilities seem to be opening. I also took Alec for sessions on an underwater treadmill, and these added up financially as well. But they were crucial to maintaining his quality of life, and increased affordability and accessibility of exercise options would greatly facilitate caregiving of animals with disabilities. The lakes had the advantage of being free, but the weather in our city was often cold and rainy, which limited our sessions, as did the fact that not all outdoor swimming spots allowed dogs. Further, all of these areas (the lake, pool, and clinic with the underwater treadmill) were a considerable drive from our home, and while I was fortunate to have a car, for those who do not, their options are even more limited due to policies that prohibit companion animals on most public transportation in the U.S. As with housing policies that discriminate against renters with companion animals, this is another instance where lack of access to societal spaces for pet guardians generally (not just specific to animals with disabilities) needs to be reformed.

Access to Public Transit

The fact that companion animals are prohibited from many social spaces amplifies the difficulties one may face when caring for a companion animal with a disability. Public policy should be changed to allow access to public transit for caretakers of companion animals, thereby reflecting their de facto status as family members for many people. Leashed and under control animals should be permitted on buses and trains when space allows. Dogs and cats are allowed to ride on many trains and buses throughout Europe, which is generally more dog-friendly than the U.S. (Euro Railways, n.d.; SNCB Europe, n.d.). Though laws vary by city and country, dogs are also more likely to be allowed inside stores, restaurants, and cafes in Europe. Access to public transportation would make it much easier for pet guardians without a car to transport their animal to the veterinarian or to accessible exercise areas.

Animal-Friendly Workplaces

Many people who would be responsible and loving caretakers are understandably reluctant to add a companion animal to their family because they work full-time and would either have to leave the animal alone all day or pay for a dog-walking service or "doggie daycare," a circumstance which makes responsible animal adoption less accessible for those who are not financially well off. This is another situation that is amplified when we consider the needs of animals with disabilities, who may have medical issues that make them unable to be left for long periods of time. To make it easier for a guardian to care for an animal who has become disabled (as well as support the human-animal bond and mitigate companion animal neglect and loneliness generally), more workplaces should adopt flexible policies regarding companion animals. This can be done in a way that takes everyone's interests into account and could be addressed by each individual place of business to assess the needs and desires of its employees and the physical constraints of the work spaces available. As an added bonus, a growing body of research shows that pets in the workplace can have positive effects on employee happiness and productivity (Valade, 2016).

Sidewalk and Street Crossing Design

Curb ramps, also addressed by the ADA (Civil Rights Division of the U.S. Department of Justice, 2009), are important for making sidewalks, street crossings, and other pedestrian routes accessible to people with disabilities. They are also vital for those caring for animals with disabilities. It is difficult and dangerous for an individual using a wheelchair or other mobility device to cross the street when the sidewalks end on either side without a curb ramp. In this situation the person with a disability, or caretaker of an animal with a disability, must make a difficult choice. They can stay home and not go to their desired destination, or they can risk their safety by entering the street and traveling alongside vehicular traffic until another curb ramp appears. Alec and I would often have to do this, using a driveway to leave the sidewalk in advance of the corner when a curb ramp wasn't present and walking in the street until we could get back up on the sidewalk.

Title II of the ADA requires state and local governments to make pedestrian crossings accessible to people with disabilities by providing curb ramps, but requirements differ based on the age of the particular street or and sidewalk (Americans with Disabilities Act Title II Regulations, 2016). If constructed before 1992 ("pre-ADA") and not altered since, state and local governments may choose to construct curb ramps, but are not necessarily required to do so

(Civil Rights Division of the U.S. Department of Justice, 2007; Civil Rights Division of the U.S. Department of Justice, 2008). This is an area of overlap between the concerns and needs of people with disabilities and caretakers of animals with disabilities. If pedestrian routes were more accessible to people, by extension they would also be to animals using mobility devices.

Information, Resources, and Support

Americans spend thousands of dollars per year on veterinary care for their companion animals (American Pet Products Association, n.d.; Thompson, 2013) because they are treasured members of the family. Veterinary professionals should act in accordance with this designation and never steer a guardian toward "euthanasia" without presenting all relevant information to the client—including letting them know when information about long-term outcomes is lacking. They should also share resources about caring for an animal with a disability and be supportive of clients who may be bewildered, overwhelmed, and uncertain about next steps in light of a life-changing circumstance but are committed to being a responsible medical advocate who makes the best decision for their friend. In this delicate and likely emotional time where a guardian may be considering "euthanasia" for their animal and relying exclusively on the trusted veterinary professional's counsel to decide next steps, it is vital that all options are presented to the caretaker, especially if indeed there is hope for a good quality of life, and that resources are offered to assist the guardian with making necessary lifestyle adjustments. This can be a difficult and confusing time for the client and care should be taken by veterinarians to present realistic information while not prematurely closing off options due to misunderstandings about disability.

In cases where there are relevant studies like the one I cited above, veterinarians should be familiar with this research and offer it to clients who express interest in learning more about their animal's condition. It can be difficult for a layperson to access academic journal articles, which if found are often not available for free download but must be purchased at significant cost. Information and research articles pertaining to companion animals with disabilities—whether relating to outcomes, therapeutic modalities, or something else—should be open-access.

Affordable Veterinary Care and Pet Insurance Options

Affordability of veterinary care would facilitate responsible guardianship for all companion animals, but especially those living with disabilities. Improvements in medical care for pets have mirrored advances in human medicine, and with them options and costs have skyrocketed. As with medical care for people—which has its own serious access problems in the U.S. that would likely need to be addressed before turning to veterinary care—no animal should be denied medical treatment or vital support services like physical therapy because it is too costly for his owner. Greater availability and affordability of pet insurance options (and expansion of coverage to include physical therapy) would also help support responsible and compassionate care for animals who become disabled. A pet owner's financial resources can quickly become depleted when the animal in her care suddenly develops serious medical needs, whether in the form of a physical impairment or chronic illness.

Education and Cultural Norms

Public education campaigns about animal behavior to raise awareness about species-specific physical, social, and psychological needs are crucial to increase animal well-being and prevent neglect. Humane education programs to teach children about the responsibility and long-term commitment involved in pet guardianship, as well as respect and appropriate behavior in the company of animals, are also beneficial. These programs could include a component on animals with disabilities to show that with appropriate care and support they can enjoy a good quality of life. Humane education programs targeted to young people are important because their attitudes and values are still forming; it is more difficult to change the behavior of adults who may have been socialized to think of pets in instrumental or objective ways. These programs should teach that, like us, animals are subjects-of-a-life (Regan, 1983) and have inherent value.

The current classification of animals as property under the law is a hindrance to their interests being taken seriously in society; companion animals with disabilities may find themselves at an even greater disadvantage. However, the law follows social change, which starts at the grassroots. As social norms about animals continue to evolve, the legal system will shift to reflect the growing cultural awareness of animals as family members whose lives have intrinsic value. Treating nonhuman members of the family with dignity and respect not only matters to those individual animals, but will also contribute to the creation of a new social consciousness and a better world for all animals.

References

Americans with Disabilities Act Title II Regulations (amended 2016, August 11). Part 35: Nondiscrimination on the basis of disability in state and local government services. Retrieved from https://www.ada.gov/regs2010/titleII_2010/titleII_2010_regulations.htm

American Pet Products Association. (n.d.). *Pet industry market size & ownership statistics.* Retrieved from http://www.americanpetproducts.org/press_industrytrends.asp

Anderson, L. (2012). Why leisure matters: Facilitating full inclusion. *Social Advocacy and Systems Change Journal, 3*(1). 1–13

ASPCA. (2016). *Shelter intake and surrender: Pet statistics.* Retrieved from http://www.aspca.org/animal-homelessness/shelter-intake-and-surrender/pet-statistics

Bradshaw, J. (2011). *Dog sense: How the new science of dog behavior can make you a better friend to your pet.* New York, NY: Basic Books.

Civil Rights Division of the U.S. Department of Justice. (2006, January-March). *Enforcing the ADA: A status report from the Department of Justice.* Retrieved from https://www.ada.gov/janmar06.htm

Civil Rights Division of the U.S. Department of Justice. (2007, August 20). *ADA guide for small towns.* Retrieved from https://www.ada.gov/smtown.htm#anchor26838

Civil Rights Division of the U.S. Department of Justice. (2008, October 9). *The ADA and city governments: Common problems.* Retrieved from https://www.ada.gov/comprob.htm.

Civil Rights Division of the U.S. Department of Justice. (2009). *ADA best practices tool kit for state and local governments.* Retrieved from https://www.ada.gov/pcatoolkit/chap6toolkit.htm

Dyschkant, A. (2015). Legal personhood: How we are getting it wrong. *University of Illinois Law Review,* 2075.

El Nasser, H. (2001, December 8). Fastest-growing urban parks are for the dogs. *USA Today.* Retrieved from http://usatoday30.usatoday.com/news/nation/story/2011-12-07/dog-parks/51715340/1.

Euro Railways (n.d.). *Traveling with dogs.* Retrieved from http://www.eurorailways.com/kb/articles/dog.htm

Favre, D. (2010). Living property: A new status for animals within the legal system. *Marquette Law Review, 93*(3), 1021.

Francione, G. (2004). *Animals, property, and the law.* Philadelphia, PA: Temple University Press.

Frasch, P. D., Katherine M., Hessler, S., Kutil, M., & Waisman, S. S. (2011). *Animal law in a nutshell.* St. Paul, MN: Thompson Reuters.

Goering, S. (2015). Rethinking disability: The social model of disability and chronic disease. *Current reviews in musculoskeletal medicine, 8*(2), 134–138.

Grimm, D. (2014). *Citizen canine: Our evolving relationship with cats and dogs.* New York, NY: Public Affairs Books.

Horn, A. (2015, May 5). City park spending, playgrounds, and dog parks are on the rise. *City Parks Blog.* Retrieved from http://cityparksblog.org/2015/05/05/city-park-spending-playgrounds-and-dog-parks-are-on-the-rise/

Huss, R. (2002). Valuing man's and woman's best friend: The moral and legal status of companion animals. *Marquette Law Review, 86*(1), 47.

Larson, K. (2016). Should pet bans be banned? Renters and landlords square off. *CBC News.* Retrieved from: https://www.cbc.ca/news/canada/british-columbia/pet-bans-rental-tenancy-laws-1.3487719

Morris, J. (2001). Impairment and disability: Constructing an ethics of care that promotes human rights. *Hypatia, 16*(4), 1–16.

Moyne, A. (2012, June 8). *Social and medical models of disability.* Retrieved from http://www.disability.ie/disability-ie-information-portal/site-sections/rights-legislation/185-society/538-social-and-medical-models-of-disability

Olby, N., Levine, J., Harris, T., Muñana, K., Skeen, T., & Sharp, N. (2003, March 15). Long-term functional outcome of dogs with severe injuries of the thoracolumbar spinal cord: 87 cases (1996–2001). *Journal of the American Veterinary Medical Association, 222*(6), 762–769.

Oliver, M. (1996). *Understanding disability: From theory to practice.* New York, NY: St. Martin's Press.

Owens, J. (2015). Exploring the critiques of the social model of disability: The transformative possibility of Arendt's notion of power. *Sociology of Health and Illness, 37*(3), 385–403.

Pallotta, N. (2016, August). *Chattel or child? The liminal status of companion animals in society and law.* Paper presented at the American sociological association annual meeting, Seattle, Washington.

Prosin, N., & Wise, S. (2014). The Nonhuman Rights Project: Coming to a country near you. *Global Journal of Animal Law, 2.*

Regan, T. (1983). *The case for animal rights.* Berkeley, CA: University of California Press.

Shakespeare, T., & Watson, N. (2002). The social model of disability: An outdated ideology? *Research in Social Science and Disability, 2,* 9–28.

Shannon-Missal, L. (2015, July 16). *More than ever, pets are members of the family.* Retrieved from http://www.theharrispoll.com/health-and-life/Pets-are-Members-of-the-Family.html

SNCB Europe. (n.d.). *On which trains are you allowed to bring your pet?* Retrieved from https://www.b-europe.com/Travel/Practical/Travel%20preparation/Pets

Stewart, M. (n.d.). Disabled renters' housing rights. *NOLO.* Retrieved from https://www.nolo.com/legal-encyclopedia/disabled-renters-housing-rights-30121.html

Sunstein, C. R., & Nussbaum, M. C. (Eds.). (2005). *Animal rights: Current debates and new directions.* New York, NY: Oxford University Press.

Taylor, R. R. (2005). Can the social model explain all of disability experience? Perspectives of persons with chronic fatigue syndrome. *American Journal of Occupational Therapy, 59*(5), 497–506.

Taylor, S. (2014). Animal crips. *Journal for Critical Animal Studies*, *12*(2), 95–117.

Terzi, L. (2004). The social model of disability: A philosophical critique. *Applied Philosophy*, *21*(2), 141–157.

Thompson, D. (2013, February 23). These 4 charts explain exactly how Americans spend $52 billion on our pets in a year. *The Atlantic*. Retrieved from: https://www.theatlantic.com/business/archive/2013/02/these-4-charts-explain-exactly-how-americans-spend-52-billion-on-our-pets-in-a-year/273446/

Valade, J. (2016). Could your office go pet-friendly? Dogs in the workplace can make employees happier and more productive. *All Animals Magazine*. The Humane Society of the United States. Retrieved from http://www.humanesociety.org/news/magazines/2016/05-06/dogs-at-work.html

Waisman, S. A., Frasch, P. D., & Wagman, B. A. (2014). *Animal law: Cases and materials (Fifth Edition)*. Durham, NC: Carolina Academic Press.

Wise, S. (2000). *Rattling the cage: Toward legal rights for animals*. New York, NY: Perseus Publishing.

8. *Seeding Ableism*

AVA HABERKORNHALM

In my community, I work within the food justice movement as an advocate for inclusion. My work includes developing an inclusive community garden; advocating for accessibility and inclusion in community growing spaces and leading workshops on inclusive food justice. Two terms significant to my work are "inclusive" and "community garden". "Inclusive" is defined as a social, emotional, and physical environment in which every individual both *feels* and *is* safe, respected and valued enough to be able to fully participate in the community gardening and food justice movements. Furthermore, the Center for Disease Control and Prevention (CDC) (2010), defines community gardens as "collaborative projects on shared open spaces where participants share in the maintenance and products of the garden, including healthful and affordable fresh fruits and vegetables" (para. 1). Additionally, community gardens are may offer opportunities for strengthening social connections, skill building, decreasing community violence, and increasing physical activity (CDC, 2010).

Building from this definition of a community garden, an *inclusive* community garden further requires that the space is not only accessible in according to the American Disabilities Act (ADA) but is also socially and emotionally welcoming. An inclusive community garden is a place where all activities are held in an accessible environment and where participants—representative of a diversity of cultures, ages, economic statuses, and abilities—share leadership roles and responsibilities.

Ableism within the Food Justice Movement

Despite growing popularity, most community gardens lack any type of accessibility—even if they are on government owned land, and are legally required to be accessible under the Americans with Disabilities Act. This widespread inaccessibility forces many community members with physical accessibility needs (per the US Census Bureau, 1 in 5 Americans are disabled (Bernstein, 2012), to be excluded from their community gardens. Furthermore, although there are more community gardens that are starting to incorporate accessible garden beds, few, if any, are also inclusive. In fact, the majority of accessible gardens, in my region, are run by medical and/or educational organizations. These gardens are what I call "special education gardens." They are primarily run by non-disabled people and marketed as inspirational learning spaces. "Special education gardens," although often ADA accessible, are built on a charity model of disability through which the disabled gardeners are treated like inspirational students and not like knowledgeable peers, farmers, and/or gardeners. It is important to note, that my knowledge of accessible/inclusive community gardens isn't exhaustive, and it is equally important to note that the rarity of these spaces across the United States, makes concrete statistics nearly impossible to gather.

I see and feel this lack of inclusive community gardens immensely. I've had the opportunity to work with many local food justice advocates, non-profit workers, and coordinators of community gardens/farms. However, to date, only one garden organization has taken concrete steps to become inclusive. It has almost become predictable, for my suggestions for accessibility and inclusion to be dismissed, not acted upon, or met with hostility. For example, I was once hired as a program manager for a gardening organization that received a grant to become inclusive. They dismissed all my ideas for accessibility, cancelled all my community classes, continued to hold board meetings in an inaccessible space, and asked me to pretend to use a walker in their fundraising video. I was a token to them—the disabled person as an inspiration.

Although, my experience with this organization was unique in the humiliation it caused, their attitude towards inclusion, itself, was not a unique experience. Often, I hear the following justifications for inaccessibility in a community growing space: lack of resources (even after I offer inexpensive, ways to make the space accessible); accessibility will negatively influence production; accessibility is a waste of time and resources because of lack of disabled participants; and/or organizations highlight the fact that they already have some disabled participants so the space is accessible enough. Although all these excuses may contain some validity, it exclusion is exclusion and exclusion is oppression. As Paulo Freire (2012) stated:

> Any situation in which "A" objectively exploits "B" or hinders his and her pursuit of self—affirmation as a responsible person is one of oppression. Such a situation

constitutes violence, even when sweetened by false generosity, because it interferes with the individual's ontological and historical vocation to be more fully human. (p. 55)

Thus, inaccessibility and non-inclusivity are barriers to participate in a movement that regards food security as a human right; a movement that sees food access as a necessity for being fully human. So, I ask you, reader, to contemplate, what these practices of exclusion (whether conscious or unconscious), tell us about who is considered human and who isn't? Why are some people welcomed to grow their own food in the community, while others can't even access the space? As Abby Wilkerson (2013) states:

> Food is much more than a means of survival; food practices, given their cultural basis, constitute an embodied manifestation of social hierarchies enacted through daily practices of exclusion and inclusion; of external control as well as self-monitoring and discipline; of producing, selling, and buying; of working and of giving and receiving care. Equally, food practices constitute an avenue for seeking justice, conviviality, a better life. (p. 106)

In order to create sustainable change, I first want to explore the deep historical and social roots of ableism to understand the ways they present today. It is necessary to view these social -behavioral patterns as rooted, firmly in our socio-political history. Understanding oppression takes the blame off the oppressed, places it on the oppressive system, and creates room for positive action. Recognizing the complex ways in oppression works to undermine equity and equality I focus on efforts that emphasize how *everything is connected*. Freire and Bergman Ramos (2012) wrote:

> Once a situation of violence and oppression has been established, it engenders an entire way of life and behavior for those caught up in it—oppressors and oppressed alike. Both are submerged in this situation, and both bear marks of oppression. Analysis of existential situations of oppression reveals that their inception lay in an act of violence—initiated by those with power. This violence, as a process, is perpetuated from generation to generation of oppressors who become its heirs and are shaped in its climate. This climate creates in the oppressor a strongly possessive consciousness—possessive of the world and of men and women. (p. 58)

The Roots: Eugenics, the Disabled Body/Mind and the Socialized Environment

Disabled people have had our exclusion from social spaces justified, and our presence in the community policed, for hundreds of years. The term *disabled* originated in the 1800s to describe impaired Civil War veterans who were considered unable to compete in the production based economy and in need social services. Institutions were, then constructed to house disabled community members, along with the "feeble minded" (the era's term for cognitively impaired), and other societal members with impairments, away from society. It was thought that disabled community members could not safely live alone, (like the thought process behind creating "special education gardens" today). However, inside the institutions, residents grew their own food, cleaned the facilities, and helped care for each other. Due to their labor, most institutions eventually became self-sufficient. Mitchell and Snyder (2010) explained:

> This designation as "non-productive" developed although many institutional residents participated in laboring economies developed within institutional societies: residents farmed the institution's land, provided housekeeping services to fellow inmates and administrators, supervised each other on behalf of the institution, produced products for the state—brooms, clothing, baskets, etc.—at excessively low wage rates. In many cases, nothing more was provided in exchange for their labors beyond the "benefit" of living an excluded life within the walls of the institution. (pp. 184–185)

Institutionalizing the disabled also marked the beginning of rehabilitation-based segregation and eugenics. Eugenics is the study of, or belief in, improving the human gene pool by either discouraging the inheritance of undesirable genetic traits (negative eugenics) or by encouraging the reproduction of highly desirable human traits (positive eugenics). The birth of eugenics, categorically separated humans into "normal" and "deviant", "worthy" and "unworthy", "humans" and "burdens." Mitchell and Synder (2010) wrote:

> By the end of the nineteenth century, efforts to segregate, restrict, and oppress populations, identified variously as "feebleminded," "subnormal," "deviant," etc., went increasingly trans-national. Eugenics, the social engineering project that sought to eradicate defective traits from a nation's hereditary pool, went global. Scientific collectives were formed, restrictive policies were translated from one cultural context to another with relative ease, categories of pathology proliferated, and parallel populations found themselves increasingly the subjects of incarceration practices. (p. 187)

Today, the discourse and/or practice of eugenics (the eradication of "bad" or "imperfect") can be still found in various social spheres such as Special Education, prenatal testing for disability, and the food justice movement. In the food justice movement, statistics on obesity, health, and disease, often accompany articles on community gardening and/ or food access and the concepts of health offered in these articles often portray disability as a symptom of poor health. Guthman (2011) offered:

> The food justice movement aims to bring analogous focus to food-related environmental conditions (e.g., food deserts) and income insufficiencies that lead to ill health. Obese bodies are evidence of injustice, with lack of access to good food assumed to be the cause. Therein lies the problem. (p. 154)

It is assumed that "health problems" are, (at least in part), due to the consumption of processed foods, or the limited consumption of fruits and vegetables. In this pattern of thought, chronically disabled people become the constant opposition of ideal physical representations within the food justice and community gardening movements, and thus, the worth our disabled body/minds are lessened. Drawing from Julie Guthman's (2011) work, we are reminded:

> Although food activists may see inequitable access to good food, as it putatively manifests in the body, as a form of oppression, others (including fat activists, disability rights activists, some queer activists, and some feminists) see the problematization of nonnormative bodies as a form of oppression. (p. 155)

Nothing exists in a vacuum. The present-day reality of disabled Americans is rooted in a history of institutionalization and eugenics. It follows, therefore, that the food justice movement with its commitment to health, would perpetuate ability-based segregation.

Inclusive Food Justice, Eco-ability and Anti-Oppression Education

Instead of food justice, therefore, I advocate for inclusive food justice and eco-ability. Inclusive food justice is rooted in solidarity and autonomy. It calls for ability, sex, gender, race, and class, to ALL be considered when engaging in activism and/or thinking critically about the environment. Inclusive food justice is as much about addressing oppressive consciousness as it is about creating inclusive spaces. Eco-ability is essential to a framework that equates eugenics of disability with eugenics of nature, and thus the liberation of both. Socha, Bentley, and Schatz (2014), quoting Nocella, Bentley, and Duncan (2012), explained:

> …Eco-ability argues for the respect of difference and diversity, challenging social constructions of what is considered normal and equal. Eco-ability also challenges labels and categories that divide and separate rather than unify and collaborate. Eco-ability respects imperfection and the value of "flaws." … Difference was, and is, the essential ingredient for human and global survival. (p. 2)

Only when framed by inclusive food justice and eco-ability principles, will the food justice movement become more equitable overall, and create sustainable, systemic, change. Drawing from Freire and Bergman Ramos, we are reminded:

> To surmount the situation of oppression, people must first critically recognize its causes, so that through transforming action they can create a new situation, one that makes possible the pursuit of a fuller humanity. (p.47)

I envision a solution in the form of an anti-oppression education and inclusive food justice cooperative. Anti-oppression education centers on the ideology and practice of connection. I define anti-oppression education as an education where: critical thinking is encouraged, spaces are accessible, there is no "normal", divergence is encouraged, and there is no dominant generalizations of the past—or of people, voices, and struggles. There is no segregation, and there are no "special needs". Anti-oppression education exists outside of privileged spaces. It consists of identifying oppression, thinking critically about oppression, healing from internalized oppression, and activism. As Freire and Bergman Ramos (2012) wrote:

> It is only when the oppressed find the oppressor out and become involved in the organized struggle for their liberation that they begin to believe in themselves. This discovery cannot be purely intellectual but must involve action; nor can it be limited to mere activism but must include serious reflection: only then will it be a praxis. (p. 65)

Growing food is also an important part of anti-oppression education. It creates personal agency, promotes unity with the external environment, and can create just communities. Food autonomy solidifies personhood.

It is naïve to think that a shift away from segregation and oppression will happen overnight. Ableism, rooted in social ideals that have been reproduced throughout centuries, will require constant unlearning by both disabled and non-disabled people. Community gardens, may seem like relatively small arenas of change, however, access to food is akin to human beings right to exist. By creating inclusive growing spaces, we can begin to resolve the conflict of the disabled body/mind vs. the social and built environment, in concrete ways. With close consideration for how ableism is too often reproduced embedded in many of the proposed actions to addressing oppression in our communities, I end this piece with a quote from Paul Longmore's (2003) *Why I Burned My Book and Other Essays on Disability*. Longmore wrote:

> Non-disabled people may question the connections that disabled people detect … Disabled activists and social scientists start from the premise that all individual

and institutional behavior towards people with disabilities ... is shaped by historically deep-seated cultural presuppositions about disability and what sort of person Americans ought to be ... They have been and are the ultimate Other ... (p. 206)

References

Bernstein, R. (2012, July 25). *Nearly 1 in 5 people have a disability in the U.S., Census Bureau Reports Report Released to Coincide with 22nd Anniversary of the ADA*. Retrieved from https://www.census.gov/newsroom/releases/archives/miscellaneous/cb12-134.html

Center for Disease Control and Prevention. (2010, June 3). Retrieved from http://www.cdc.gov/healthyplaces/healthtopics/healthyfood/community.htm

Freire, P. (2012). *Pedagogy of the oppressed (30th anniversary ed.)* (M. Bergman Ramos, Trans.). New York, NY: Bloomsbury Academic.

Guthman, J. (2011). *Weighing in: Obesity, food justice, and the limits of capitalism*. Berkeley and Los Angeles, CA: University of California Press.

Longmore, P. K. (2003). *Why I burned my book and other essays on disability*. Philadelphia, PA: Temple University Press.

Mitchell, D. T., & Snyder, S. L. (2010, May 1). Disability as multitude: Re-working non-productive labor power. *Journal of Literary and Cultural Disability Studies, 4*(2), 179–194. doi:10.3828/jlcds.2010.14

Nocella II, A. J., Bentley, K. C., & Duncan J. (2012). Introduction: The rise of eco-ability. In A. J. Nocella II, K. C. Bentley, & J. Duncan (Eds.), *Earth, animal, and disability liberation: The rise of the eco-ability movement* (pp. xiii–xxii). New York, NY: Peter Lang Publishing.

Socha, K. A., Bentley, J. K., & Schatz, J. (2014, May). An introduction to eco-ability: The struggle for justice, with focus on humans with disabilities and nonhuman animals. *Journal for Critical Animal Studies, 12*(2), 1–8. Retrieved from http://www.criticalanimalstudies.org/wp-content/uploads/2014/04/JCAS-Vol-12-Issue-2-May-20145.pdf

Wilkerson, A. (2013). A place at the table. *The Philosophers' Magazine*, 2nd Quarter (61), 100–106.

9. Dealing with Trauma Holistically: Introducing Eco-ability Liberatory Therapy

MARISSA ANDERSON

Introduction

While examining the experiences of people suffering from traumatic memories, it is important to incorporate aspects of the natural world into any treatment plan designed to help individuals recover. Many people who have endured trauma and subsequent recurrent memories, often develop thought suppression or trying to eliminate thoughts, ideas, and images related to undesirable stimulus (Matlin, 2013, p. 91) as a defense mechanism. A more effective, healthy and productive way to deal with traumatic memories is to have a well-rounded therapy treatment plan. In this chapter, I will define and introduce eco-ability liberatory therapy. I argue that eco-ability will not only help humans with their trauma, but also aid in the destruction of oppression and dismantle capitalism, which in return help all beings and Nature be liberated from systemic oppression. In this chapter, I will begin by introducing myself because locating oneself is a socio-political perspective known as feminist standpoint methodology (Harding, 2003). Feminist standpoint theory is a critical, activist-scholarly theory in which the author explains and defends their choice to write personally about a topic to which they are an expert. Feminist standpoint theory is particularly relevant to this discussion since it argues that all scholars, researchers, and theory are subjective and no one or no theory can be objective, apolitical and detached (Harding, 2003).

Locating Myself

I am an intersectional feminist with mental disabilities, who is also a vegan, anarchist, Hip Hop activist, and defender of the Earth and all its inhabitants. Who I am allows me to engage in a mutual liberation between the environment and myself. It is mutual liberation in that I fight to defend the Earth against human exploitation and the Earth in return allows me to feel free, liberated, and at peace when I sit next to a river, hike up a mountain, or ride my bike on a path through the forest. The Earth provides everything that human and nonhuman animals need while it continues to be exploited for financial gain by humans. The capitalistic society that has been created by human animals has caused destruction for all living things (Best & Nocella, 2006). Once a person has the experience of liberating the environment, they can then have the Earth liberate them back, but it is important to remember that the Earth does not belong to us, rather, we belong to the Earth. We must remember that Earth is our home that we dwell on and Earth does not need us to exist, but we need the Earth to exist.

As someone who identifies as an Earth activist, I joined the Sioux tribe and other water protectors at Standing Rock to protect Mother Earth. We engaged in a direct action on "thanksgiving" that is now known as one of the biggest demonstrations to take place on the front lines of Native land. During the protests, I rode in a rowboat holding my "NO Dakota Access Pipeline" sign with two other activists from Fort Lewis College chanting "Water is Life," and "you can't drink oil, keep it in the soil," and "Who do you stand for? Mother Earth! Who do you stand with? Standing Rock." I felt the splashes of the water I was defending and the breeze of thankfulness from Mother Earth. To exploit the planet that has given us so much is disrespectful, as we should view this relationship no different than how we see the relationship between humans, where one individual is thankful and gives back to those that have given to them. This is an example of mutual friendship and should not be limited to only human relationships. This friendship is valuable to all life.

When activists defend the Earth and all that live on it, they support themselves. The Earth naturally provides us with air, water and fire, and all of the other elements we need in order to survive. It is our responsibility to provide the Earth with what she needs to survive, and currently she needs protection against destruction caused by exploitative humans. Our loved ones live on the Earth, and if we can be thankful and work and protect her, it is likely we can then live in a healthy, beautiful, global, diverse, and complex ecosystem that we can appreciate. We have gotten away from being one with the Earth through the use of technology and reliance on capitalism. When breaking away from this harmonious, holistic, and interdependent relationship between human animals and the Earth, we give up, the idea of what it means to value life, love, liberation, and freedom. With the recognition of Mother Earth as a powerful woman, and the one who started the family tree, it is vital that we recognize the love, respect and defending she needs.

When discussing Mother Earth, you must also mention the creatures that live on her. Part of liberating Mother Earth requires liberating its animals, human and nonhuman alike. As a college student and Earth activist, I spend time disseminating literature about animal liberation and attending conferences such as the 15th Annual North American Conference for Critical Animal Studies held at Fort Lewis College. This creates a space for me to learn, educate, experience and organize with others around veganism and animal liberation, which is important for many reasons. To have liberated, knowledgeable and passionate people around you while working to liberate animals and Mother Earth makes social justice more likely to be achieved. This community will aid in your understanding as well as push you to continue in your work. The process of community building helps one become more responsible because you are more likely to be held accountable for your actions. It is also nice to be supported during times of struggle and persecution. One is more likely to feel strong and liberated when one realizes that you are not alone in the recognition of this struggle and others want to help liberate Mother Earth and animals as well.

As an eco-ability activist-scholar, I work to liberate nonhuman animals using a vegan framework. This means not eating nonhuman animals, or utilizing anything made from or by animals. If we want to liberate nonhuman animals, we must promise that human animals will help them, not hurt them. When we recognize the way that nonhuman animals are tortured and exploited in institutionalized settings such as factory farms, we can better understand why we should go vegan (Kirby, 2010). By allowing nonhuman animals to be treated in ways that would be considered cruel to human animals, we are speciesist. Thus, adopting a vegan lifestyle both in mind and body means that human animals must put aside their normalized beliefs about the necessity to eat meat and drink dairy in order to liberate and respect nonhumans, while at the same time perpetuating a healthier planet, body, and mind (Lyman, 2001).

When it comes to the physical benefits of adopting a vegan diet, it can allow the human body to work in its most natural state (Robbins, 1987). For instance, milk products that derive from the species mother are healthy for their babies. However, consuming milk is not a lifelong dietary need for any species. In fact, humans are the only species that intake milk their entire lives, and drink the milk of another mammal entirely. Thus, consuming milk products is not only unnecessary but artificial in terms of natural processes. When one adopts a vegan lifestyle and promises to stop ingesting another mammal's milk, they allow that milk to be used for what it is meant: The baby of that cow (Baur, 2008). Liberation of animals starts with respecting their life and bodies which entail not stealing their milk or inseminating female cows artificially to produce milk products unnecessarily. With an intersectional framework it is also easy to see that this is exploitation of women.

The spiritual and ethical benefits of adopting a vegan diet include embracing the idea that nonhuman animals are friends, not food. Some cite the hypocrisy of eating mass produced cow, pig, turkey, and chicken flesh for protein when dog or cat meat are never on American's menus. Others suggest that there are other ways to obtain proteins by eating soy, beans, leafy green vegetables, quinoa, and seeds instead of eating the flesh of other species. Disability studies argues against creating a hierarchy of value on difference, rather seeing all differences equally valuable and needed in a healthy interdependent relationship we call an ecosystem. Total liberation argues that if one species is oppressed, we are all oppressed, similar to the analogy that we are only as strong as the weakest link in a chain. By helping humans understand that nonhuman animals should not be used at our disposal and that giving our bodies non-animal based foods, we ultimately aid in the liberation of our Earth, its inhabitants, and ourselves.

Overview of Eco-ability

First discussed in Anthony J. Nocella II's dissertation, eco-ability is the interweaving of animal, disability, and environmental justice and liberation together (Nocella II, 2011). Eco-ability is influenced by critical pedagogy, environmental justice, ecopedagogy, intersectionality, and critical animal studies and fundamentally grounded in the theoretical study of disability and experiences of those with disabilities for total liberation (Nocella II, White, & Cudworth, 2015). Eco-ability aims to emancipate nonhuman animals, those with disabilities (human and nonhuman animals), and the environment (Socha, Bentley, & Schatz, 2014) from oppression caused by ecocide, speciesism, and ableism. It does this by challenging the systemic nature of normalcy, which is the process by which individuals are conditioned to be "normal" (Nocella II, 2011). Eco-ability also challenges the socially constructed binaries of humans versus animals (challenged by critical animal studies), normal versus abnormal (challenged by disability studies), and domestic versus wild (environmental studies). Anarchists would define this liberatory relationship as "mutual aid" coined by theorist Peter Kropotkin (2014). Mutual aid is an economic margining system that uses the communal practices of interdependency to critique concepts such as competition, individualism, and property (i.e., the ownership of anything and anyone). To connect anarchism and eco-ability more directly together, Noam Chomsky, a prominent modern anarchist theorist, argues a humanist perspective that nonhuman animals cannot have culture and therefore cannot have language, hence cannot be part of mutual aid that already exists among humans (Singer, 2011). Chomsky's assertions were refuted by the work of Herbert S. Terrace and Thomas Bever of Columbia University who proved that chimpanzees, in particular, one individual named Nem Chimpsky, do have language and could use American Sign Language to communicate with humans (Hale, 2011). Therefore, even anarchists need to be challenged on their anthropocentric world view, which is speciesist.

Eco-ability Liberatory Therapy

Where eco-ability liberatory theory promotes mutual aid in the form of interdependency, ecotherapy focuses on caring for humans with disabilities, yet ignores caring for nature or nonhuman animals suffering due to capitalism, colonialism, and human supremacy (Jensen, 2016). Ecotherapy does, however, challenge the pharmaceutical industrial complex and the use of medicine, but does so for the betterment of human health which does nothing to end nonhuman animal testing, vivisecting, or environmental destruction (Baird & Rosenbaum, 1991). Ecotherapy also commonly uses animals such as dogs, cats, horses and even dolphins as therapeutic tools to communicate with those who have mental disabilities (Nocella, Bentley, & Duncan, 2012). While this has proven to aid those with disabilities, it is often at the expense of exploiting nonhuman animals, who are forced into these situations involuntarily. These animals used to provide services are not companies, but rather living beings that are forced to work for human animals with disabilities, often twenty-four hours a day, seven days a week, with no respite. Thus, eco-ability therapy departs from ecotherapy because it does not promote the use of nonhumans in any relationship by which mutual aid is not reciprocated in practice and theory. Eco-ability therapy seeks treatment plans in which both parties benefit and no one is forced into non-consensual relationships.

Eco-ability theory is rooted in the values of difference and diversity, holistic transformation through dialogue and education, inclusive social justice and total liberation, intersectional politics, anti-oppression, critical theory and interdependence (Nocella II et al., 2012). Eco-ability stresses that connecting with nature and the world that surrounds us, may unite one with the things one longs for. In my experience as an Earth liberationist, I struggle to live in big cities due to my mental disabilities. When I am without the opportunity to connect with the world around me, my disabilities often overpower my feelings of success and wellbeing. In a city of almost 900,000 individuals, I can feel as though I'm alone mostly because I lose touch with the Earth that helps me feel whole. Humans are meant to be in touch with the natural world around them, and when this world is consumed by big buildings, highways, pollution and the struggle to find any land that has not been colonized, people can become depressed, stressed, angry, and emotionally distressed. Over time, colonialism and capitalism has led humans to feel disconnected from nature and nonhuman animals in their natural habitats, which separates through socially constructed binaries nature from humans and nonhuman animals from human animals (Nocella II et al., 2012).

Capitalism by definition, cannot be ethical, as it requires exploiting resources, which includes humans and nonhumans, to the max to be fully efficient in fostering profit. Under a capitalist economic system, all individuals have a value, which can be best determined through individual competition. Eco-ability not only challenges capitalism and normalcy, but is an active force in destroying both of them. Moreover, eco-ability supports collaboration and interdependency, not competition and individualism. Eco-ability also promotes difference and equity, not sameness and equality. In a framework that embraces equity instead of equality, there is focus on the needs of an individual, instead of assuming that each person needs the same thing. This can be revolutionary to individuals who need eco-ability liberatory therapy as all people have different trauma and different disabilities. Finally, eco-ability advocates for the end of all forms of oppression and domination, specifically toward nonhuman animals and the Earth.

Capitalism perpetuates greed and competition among humans to achieve more material goods such as cars, jewelry, televisions, clothes, shoes, hats, jackets, watches, and homes (Kovel, 2002). Under capitalism, everything is based on monetary value; therefore, whoever is the wealthiest and has the most stuff, is the most successful. When our understanding of life can only be defined by who owns what and what is owned, we allow capitalism to control the empathy and compassion we have for all of life. Under this type of socio-economic arrangement, it is very easy to lose perspective on what is important. For example, humans cut down trees to make more money, but they do not water the trees that are standing to give us clean air. This is ecocide and dangerous to all inhabitants of the Earth (Churchill, 2002).

Capitalism has all inhabitants of Mother Earth, conscious or not, trapped in a system that is exploitative, but it is desired by human society, specifically those in power (Kahn, 2010). One that has us hating each other and hating ourselves. To keep up with the pressures of life, capitalism has us focused on gaining employment that will pay the most, and will have the best benefits, instead of allowing us to do what our hearts and bodies need and want to do. We have our hobbies on the side instead of at the forefront, because some of them don't pay as well. Our entire day is spent being productive as cogs in a machine that promotes competition and individualism.

However, once we stop to reflect on how busy capitalism has made us, and how it fundamentally forces us to categorize the Earth's resources into property that needs to be owned, sold or destroyed for profit, we can see just how harmful it is for us (Zerzan, 2002). Moreover, we have become cogs in an economic system that defines success as the maximization of exploitation of a resource and labor. If we can recognize the harm that we are doing by exploiting Earth, nonhuman animals, and subsequently marginalized human groups, then we can recognize like anarchists do, that property is theft (Proudhon, 1840) and the significance of fighting systems of oppression. This system does not need reform; it needs abolishment. This system of oppression was built for only for able-bodied and minded, academically educated, employed, wealthy, Christian, heterosexual, white, male, human animals to succeed and as such it is a system that either ignores or exploits many other living organisms.

Furthermore, since so many humans live away from the natural world, this makes it even more imperative that eco-ability liberatory therapy encourage some interaction with nature. Some holistic and sustainable interactions might include a hike in the forest, surf in the ocean, swim in a lake, raft down a river, or climb a mountain. According to the eco-ability framework, engaging with nature is necessary to being a whole human being and earthling, which is an interdependent member within the global ecosystem. Participating in activities in nature, as noted above, is a therapeutic way of utilizing eco-ability, and also giving back to the Earth and its inhabitants by being a good steward of the land. Eco-ability liberatory therapy encourages individuals to spend time nurturing the Earth, and while doing this, also learning how to take part in a mutual aid relationship. Education is liberation, and being able to understand how you can help the eco-system is a way of caring for something outside of yourself which has the potential to be effective with people who have trauma. I have experienced this in Durango, Colorado as well as in Standing Rock away from the capitalist, competitive, industrial, non-spiritual, corporate urban society. Despite the lack of literature explaining how trauma patients can benefit by taking care of nonhumans, I have witnessed that individuals who care for others outside of themselves often feel better because they are more physically active. On the contrary, I have also witnessed that individuals with disabilities that have service and companion nonhuman animals sometimes feel more stress because it's often difficult to keep up with the work of caring for them.

While part of eco-ability liberatory therapy involves liberating the environment and nonhuman animals, it is important to note that these actions can also help liberate the self. In a 2010 study based on exploring "moral thought," it was found that those who state they care for others, actually rank themselves higher in moral aptitude. In other words, those who claim responsibility for caring for a child, an elder, or a pet, for instance, perceive themselves as more ethical. These individuals tend to have a higher regard for themselves (Forsyth, 2010). This plays an important role in healing for those who have experienced intense trauma. Individuals who have undergone trauma sometimes believe they deserved what happened to them, thus inferring that they do not think very highly of themselves or feel the need to blame themselves. From experience, I can say that this is not a productive way to live life. It tears you down mentally and physically and makes you feel as though there is no self-worth. Eco-ability liberatory therapy has the potential to help many individuals with trauma.

Conclusion

Eco-ability is one of the most needed interventions for Earth and animal liberation movements, as it is against greenwashing, promotes micro-reformist campaigns, and strategies that do little, but promote a so-called ethical-capitalism. It is time for capitalism and all of the hierarchies to fade, or we will perish. In conclusion, I argue that this is exactly why eco-ability liberatory therapy is the answer to many people in their struggle to emancipate themselves and the Earth. By freeing the Earth and nonhuman animals, we give ourselves the hope to be freed and self-determining.

References

Baird, R. M., & Rosenbaum, S. E. (1991). *Animal experimentation: The moral issues.* Amherst, NY: Prometheus Books.

Baur, G. (2008). *Farm sanctuary: Changing hearts and minds about animals and food.* New York, NY: Touchstone.

Best, S., & Nocella II, A. J. (2006). *Igniting a revolution: Voices in defense of the Earth*. Oakland, CA: AK Press.

Churchill, W. (2002). *Struggle for the land: Native North American resistance to genocide, ecocide, and colonization*. San Francisco, CA: City Lights Publishing.

Forsyth, D. R. (2010). *Moral attribution and the evaluation of action* (Doctoral dissertation). Retrieved from https://archive.org/details/moralattribution00fors

Hale, B. (2011). *The sad story of Nim Chimsky*. Retrieved from https://www.dissentmagazine.org/online_articles/the-sad-story-of-nim-chimpsky

Harding, S. (2003). *The feminist standpoint theory reader: Intellectual and political controversies*. New York, NY: Routledge.

Jensen, R. (2016). *The myth of human supremacy*. New York, NY: Seven Stories Press.

Kahn, R. (2010). *Critical pedagogy, ecoliteracy, and planetary crisis: The ecopedagogy movement*. New York, NY: Peter Lang Publishing.

Kirby, D. (2010). *Animal factory: The looming threat of industrial pig, dairy, and poultry farms to humans and the environment*. New York, NY: St. Martin's Press.

Kovel, J. (2002). *The enemy of nature: The end of capitalism or the end of nature?* New York, NY: Zed Books.

Kropotkin, P. (2014). *Mutual aid: A factor in evolution*. North Charleston, SC: CreateSpace.

Lyman, H. F. (2001). *Mad cowboy: Plain truth from the cattle rancher who won't eat meat*. New York, NY: Scribner.

Matlin, M. W. (2013). *Cognition* (8th ed.). Hoboken, NJ: Wiley.

Nocella II, A. J. (2011). *A Dis-ability perspective on the stigmatization of dissent: Critical pedagogy, critical criminology, and critical animal studies* (Doctoral dissertation). Retrieved from http://surface.syr.edu/socsci_etd/178/

Nocella II, A. J., Bentley, J. K. C., & Duncan, J. (2012). *Earth, animal, and disability liberation: The rise of the eco-ability movement*. New York, NY: Peter Lang Publishing.

Nocella II, A. J., White, R., & Cudworth, E. (2015). *Anarchism and animal liberation: Essays on complementary elements of total liberation*. Jefferson, NC: McFarland.

Proudhon, P. J. (1840). What is property? An inquiry into the principle of right and of government. Auckland: Floating Press.

Robbins, J. (1987). *Diet for a new America*. Walpole, NH: Stillpoint Publishing.

Singer, P. (2011). *The troubled life of Nim Chimsky*. Retrieved from http://www.nybooks.com/daily/2011/08/18/troubled-life-nim-chimpsky/

Socha, K., Bentley, J. K. C., & Schatz, J. L. (2014). An introduction to eco-ability: The struggle for justice, with focus on humans with disabilities and nonhuman animals. *Journal for Critical Animal Studies, 12*(2), 1–8.

Zerzan, J. (2002). *Running on emptiness: The pathology of civilization*. Los Angeles, CA: Feral House.

Contributors

Sarah R. Adams is an undergraduate student at Fort Lewis College, majoring in Sociology with a minor in Psychology. Adams also has also taken relevant course work in Environmental Sciences and Gender and Women's Studies. Following the completion of her bachelor's degree, Adams plans to attend graduate school to purse a master's degree in Education. Her passions include advocating for environmental sustainability and the pursuit of social justice. Adams devotes much of her time during the week to provide childcare for elementary students, volunteering for the FLC grub hub, and working on projects regarding clean and accessible water for all.

Marissa Anderson is a nontraditional undergraduate student at Fort Lewis College studying psychology and criminology. She was born in Fresno, California and raised in San Francisco and Oakland, California. The community she comes from has been impacted by police brutality and the war on drugs, which has sculpted how she feels about the criminal injustice system. She is a community organizer and activist focusing on prison abolition, animal liberation, disability justice, Earth liberation, racial and economic justice, queer liberation, Hip Hop activism, youth justice, and anarchism. She currently works full-time as a case worker at a local homeless shelter in Durango, Colorado, and volunteers doing group-building activities and poetry workshops with Save the Kids at Denier Juvenile Detention Facility.

Judy K.C. Bentley, Ph.D., is an Associate Professor at the State University of New York Cortland, in the Department of Foundations and Social Advocacy, and Director of the SUNY Cortland Institute for Disability Studies. Dr. Bentley is the founding Editor-in-Chief of *Social Advocacy and Systems Change*, a peer-reviewed, web-based journal. Recent publications include "Deconstructing Symbolic Identities and Building on Eco-ability: Expanding the Domain of Environmental Justice" in A. Nocella, A. George, & J. L. Schatz (Eds.). (2017). *The Intersectionality of Critical Animal, Disability, and Environmental Studies: Toward Eco-ability, Justice and Liberation.* Lanham, MD: Lexington. Dr. Bentley teaches courses in disability studies, research methods and inclusive special education.

Mary Fantaske is currently on disability/sick leave from her Communication and Culture Masters program at Ryerson and York Universities, but is still working on her thesis at a pace which respects her body's needs. She was originally interested in the intersectionality between sexism and speciesism, but since struggling with her own health, which has resulted in her need for mobility aids, she began noticing more and more the discriminatory ways in which persyns with disabilities are treated in our society, in addition to the commonalities between such cultural behaviour, and the way in which nonhuman persyns are treated. In addition to working on her thesis, Mary runs a casual social justice blog, which focuses on ableist, speciesist, and feminist issues, and co-organizes events and various social media for the grassroots Toronto Save animal liberation groups which "bear witness" to nonhuman persyns in their last moments before they enter the slaughterhouse. "Bearing witness" is a Tolstoian concept where, when one encounters an individual in pain, instead of giving in to the initial desire to flee, one instead brings themselves as close as possible to the persyn who is suffering, and helps in any way they can. For the Toronto Save groups this means offering the comforts of water and love to those trapped in transport vehicles parked outside Toronto's slaughterhouses.

Amber E. George, Ph.D., is a scholar-activist who teaches philosophy at Galen College. She has taught undergraduate courses in social philosophy and presented her research at many colleges and universities. She has also acquired real-life experience as an ally, counselor, and community educator in social justice administration. Dr. George is a member of the Eco-ability Collective and Executive Director of Finance of the Institute for Critical Animal Studies (ICAS). She is also the editor of *Journal of Critical Animal Studies*. She is working on writing many books and book chapters about non/human animal liberation, disability studies, and critical theory. In her spare time, she enjoys spending time with her growing family, watching television, and gardening.

Ava HaberkornHalm identifies as a disabled woman, activist, and garden enthusiast. She has given workshops and presentations on Community Gardening and Inclusive Food Justice events throughout Michigan and in Chicago. Ava, also, coordinates one of the few universally—designed community gardens in the nation, the "Better Together" Community Garden at the Ann Arbor Center for Independent Living. A Disability Rights Activist for thirteen years, Ava roots much of her work and message in her own lived experience. For more information about the Inclusive Food Justice Education Network, please visit www.facebook.com/foodjustice4all.

John Lupinacci teaches pre-service teachers and graduate students in the Cultural Studies and Social Thought in Education (CSSTE) program using an anarchist approach that advocates for the development of scholar-activist educators. He has taught at the secondary level in Detroit and is co-author of the book *EcoJustice Education: Toward Diverse, Democratic, and Sustainable Communities* (2015). His experiences as a high school math and science teacher, an outdoor environmental educator, and a community activist all contribute to examining the relationships between schools and the reproduction of the cultural roots of social suffering and environmental degradation.

Hannah Monroe is in the beginning stages of her thesis in the Master of Arts in Critical Sociology at Brock University. She is in her first year in the program and wants to study neurodiverse people in the animal rights movement. She is interested in post-structuralist and queer perspectives on neurodiversity. After completing this degree at Brock University, she is planning to get a degree in social work or counseling to become a therapist. She wants to work with individuals, especially neurodiverse and LGBTQIA people, to empower authenticity in identity.

Anthony J. Nocella II, Ph.D., award-winning author and community organizer, is Assistant Professor of Criminal Justice, Justice Studies, and Criminology in the Institute of Public Safety and the Department of Criminal Justice at Salt Lake Community College. He is the editor of the *Peace Studies Journal*, the *Transformative Justice Journal*, and the book series Poetry Behind the Walls, along with being a co-editor of five book series including Critical Animal Studies and Theory with Lexington Books and Hip Hop Studies and Activism with Peter Lang Publishing. He is the National Coordinator of Save the Kids, Executive Director of the Institute for Critical Animal Studies, and Director of the Academy for Peace Education. He has published over fifty peer-reviewed book chapters or articles and over forty books. He has been interviewed by *Houston Chronicle*, *Durango Herald*, *Fresno Bee*, *Los Angeles Times*, *Washington Post*, CNN, CBS, Fox, and *New York Times*.

Nicole R. Pallotta is the student programs coordinator for the Animal Legal Defense Fund (ALDF) and an integral member of ALDF's Animal Law Program, which is dedicated to the development of animal law in academia and legal practice. Prior to joining ALDF, Nicole completed her Ph.D. in sociology at the University of Georgia, where she developed and taught the school's first Animals and Society course. Her writing has appeared in *Sociological Perspectives, Society and Animals, The Journal for Critical Animal Studies, The Portland Tribune*, and *Animal Wellness Magazine*. She lives in Portland with her rescued dog Teagan and blogs at www.alec-story.com.

Daniel Salomon has an MA in Research from Andover Newton Theological School with Graduate Certificate in Science and Religion from Boston Theological Institute. BS Cum Laude in Liberal Studies from Salisbury University with concentrations in Biology, Environmental Studies and Conflict Analysis/Dispute Resolution, along with a Naturalist Certificate from the Au Sable Institute of Environmental Studies. Salomon is author of six books on the environment (five of them available on Amazon) and has published in the Society for Disability Studies, The Journal of Critical Animal Studies, The Scavenger, all-creatures.org and Hoyt Arboretum.

Meneka Repka, Ph.D., is an instructor at Alberta College of Art and Design. Her current research questions the neutrality of curricular discourse in Alberta by examining how dominant interests in the meat industry influence schools. Prior to completing doctoral studies, she worked as a high school and junior high teacher. Meneka's research interests include: animal liberation, critical/radical animal studies, environmental sustainability, environmental education, discourse analysis, youth activism, and social justice education.

Index

A

ability, xi, 1, 6, 13, 17, 19, 20, 27, 31, 33, 45, 53, 66, 67, 75, 79, 85, 92
ableism, xii, 2, 6, 7, 11–14, 16, 21–22, 43, 61, 67, 69, 72, 73, 75, 79, 103, 105, 107–108, 114
abnormal, 14, 64, 67, 114
academia, 11
academics, 11, 14, 15
accessibility, 95, 103–105
activism, xii, 1, 6, 10–11, 15–16, 19–21, 26, 29–30, 32–36, 45, 51, 59, 72, 79, 107–108
anarchism, 10–11, 115
animal liberation, 10, 15, 18, 41, 42, 44, 113–117
Animal Liberation Front, 12
animal rights, 18, 19, 66, 77
animal studies, 11
animal testing, 14, 16, 115
anthropocentrism, 2, 5, 13, 45–46, 83, 115
autism 6, 46, 48, 59, 61–68

B

Black Lives Matter, 9, 21
Black Panther Party, 12

C

Canada, 21
canine, 7, 18, 83, 87, 95
capitalism, 2, 31–32, 35, 46, 61, 111, 113, 115–118
carbon footprint, 48
Cartesian dualism, 13
Cats, 68–69, 75, 95, 115
Christian, 14, 27, 43, 45, 53, 56–57, 117
civilization, 11, 13, 28, 31–32, 35, 40, 44
classism, 11, 19, 43
colonialism, 17, 20, 22, 32, 41, 115, 116
community garden, 103
crip, 39
critical animal studies, ix, 1, 6, 9, 10, 59, 66–67, 114
critical disability studies, 13, 39, 43, 44, 59–60, 66
critical environmental studies, 39, 43, 47
critical pedagogy, 5, 114
critical theory, 17, 115

D

Dakota Access Pipeline, 6, 26, 28
deep ecology, 6, 39–41, 43
digital activism, 20–21
direct action, 12, 28, 34, 112

disability studies, xi, 60, 67, 93, 114
discourse(s), 13, 44, 59–69, 106
diversity, 1–2, 4, 6–7, 13, 29, 42, 59, 66, 103, 107, 115
domination, 2, 5, 10–11, 16, 56, 116
dog, 14, 18, 31, 82–92, 94–96, 114
dualism, 13

E

ecocide, 16, 114
ecocrisis, 33–35
ecofeminism, 6, 29, 41–43, 73
ecopedagogy, 25–26, 30, 33–36, 114
ecopsychology, 43
elder, 28, 33, 118
enlightenment, 44, 46, 51
environment, xii, 7, 18, 25–27, 29–30, 32–33, 35, 42, 45–46, 54, 82, 93, 103, 105, 107–108
environmental justice, 19, 39, 41–45, 114
environmental psychology, 25, 36
environmental studies, 16, 39, 43, 47
environmentalism, 41–43, 45
equality, 105, 116
equity, 105, 116

F

factory farming, 14, 21, 31–32
feminist standpoint theory, 2–5, 9, 111
food justice, 19, 21, 103–104, 106–108
food security, 105

G

garden, 7, 20, 56, 103–104, 106–108
gender, 4, 5, 27–28, 60–62, 66, 107
genocide, 13

H

heteronormative, 19
heterosexual, 1, 10, 14, 72, 117

homelessness, 78
homogenization, 46

I

ideology, 13–14, 35, 72, 83, 108
imperialism, 20, 39, 41, 43, 46
inaccessibility, 39, 104–105
inclusion, 15–16, 30, 84, 103–105
inclusive, xi-xii, 1, 3, 7, 10, 14, 17, 19, 21, 46, 103–104, 107–108, 115
Indigenous, 21, 43
individualism, 43, 46, 55, 74, 115–117
Industrial Revolution, 46
injustice, xii, 11, 15, 17, 19, 21, 45, 107
interdependency, 1, 6, 13, 16, 27, 29, 74, 115–116
intersectional, xii, 7. 10–12, 17, 20, 112, 114–115
IQ testing, 5

L

Lakota, 28
LGBTQIA, 59

M

medicalization, 6, 59, 62
media, 15, 18, 26, 35, 64
methodology, 3–5, 111
mental illness, 3, 15

N

Native American, 27–29
nature, 1–2, 4, 6–7, 11–13, 17, 25–36, 41–42, 44, 46, 51, 72–74, 79, 92–93, 107, 111, 114–117
nature deficiency, 25–26, 32–34
neurodiversity, 6, 39–40, 43. 46–48, 59–60, 63–68
normalcy, xii, 1–2, 7, 13, 15–17, 29, 39, 43, 47, 59, 61–63, 65–66, 68–69, 74, 114, 116

norms, 12, 34, 59–63, 65–68, 84, 98
normativity, 6, 59, 61, 65

O

objectification, 16–17, 71, 74–76
oppression, 2, 5, 9–12, 15, 17, 19, 22, 31, 39, 42, 47, 60–61, 66–67, 74–76, 79, 104–105, 107–108, 111, 114–117

P

patriarchy, 41
prenatal testing, 106
privilege, xii, 5, 10, 19–20, 22, 61, 63
property, 32, 81, 83–84, 94, 98, 115, 117
psychology, 15, 25, 36, 39, 43, 45

Q

queer, 5, 9, 14–15, 107

R

radical animal studies, 6
radical activism, 34
race, 5, 6, 18, 27, 61, 107
racism, xii, 6, 11–12, 14, 16–17, 19–22, 28, 44

S

sexism, xxi, 11, 28
sexuality, 27, 61
Sioux, 26–27, 112
slavery, 21
social change, 76, 98
social justice, xii, 1–2, 9, 12, 17, 22, 26, 44, 64, 76, 113, 115
social media, 10, 17, 20–21
sociology, 36
speciesism, xii, 6, 11, 16, 44, 46, 67, 69, 72–73, 75, 79, 114
Standing Rock, 6, 26–28, 33, 35, 112, 117
stigma, 14–15, 31, 62, 68

V

vivisection, 115
veganism, 18–22, 113

W

water, 26–27, 33, 35, 52, 74, 77, 83, 86–88, 112, 116
wild, 14, 17, 44, 46, 114
wilderness, 11, 41, 44, 52–57

Z

Zapatista, 12
zoo, 14–15, 18, 53

RADICAL ANIMAL STUDIES AND TOTAL LIBERATION

Anthony J. Nocella II, SERIES EDITOR

The **Radical Animal Studies and Total Liberation** book series branches out of Critical Animal Studies (a field co-founded by Anthony J. Nocella II) with the argument that criticism is not enough. Action must follow theory. This series demands that scholars are engaged with their subjects both theoretically and actively via radical, revolutionary, intersectional action for total liberation. Founded in anarchism, the series provides space for scholar-activists who challenge authoritarianism and oppression in their many daily forms. **Radical Animal Studies and Total Liberation** promotes accessible and inclusive scholarship that is based on personal narrative as well as traditional research, and is especially interested in the advancement of interwoven voices and perspectives from multiple radical, revolutionary social justice groups and movements such as Black Lives Matter, Idle No More, Earth First!, the Zapatistas, ADAPT, prison abolition, LGBTTQQIA rights, disability liberation, Earth Liberation Front, Animal Liberation Front, political prisoners, radical transnational feminism, environmental justice, food justice, youth justice, and Hip Hop activism.

To order other books in this series please contact our Customer Service Department:

(800) 770-LANG (within the US)
(212) 647-7706 (outside the US)
(212) 647-7707 FAX

To find out more about the series or browse a full list of titles, please visit our website:

WWW.PETERLANG.COM

www.ingramcontent.com/pod-product-compliance
Ingram Content Group UK Ltd.
Pitfield, Milton Keynes, MK11 3LW, UK
UKHW022240230426
12048UKWH00018BA/1367